WORLD WAR II
BATTLE BY BATTLE

OSPREY
PUBLISHING

WORLD WAR II
BATTLE BY BATTLE

NIKOLAI BOGDANOVIC

OSPREY PUBLISHING
Bloomsbury Publishing Plc

Kemp House, Chawley Park, Cumnor Hill, Oxford OX2 9PH, UK
29 Earlsfort Terrace, Dublin 2, Ireland
1385 Broadway, 5th Floor, New York, NY 10018, USA
Email: info@ospreypublishing.com
www.ospreypublishing.com

OSPREY is a trademark of Osprey Publishing Ltd

First published in Great Britain in 2019

In the compilation of this volume we relied on the following previously published Osprey titles: ACM 1: *Battle of Britain 1940*, CAM 62: *Pearl Harbor 1941*, CAM 81: *Iwo Jima 1945*, CAM 96: *Okinawa 1945*, CAM 100: *D-Day 1944 (1)*, CAM 107: *Poland 1939*, CAM 115: *Battle of the Bulge 1944 (1)*, CAM 134: *Cassino 1944*, CAM 137: *Saipan & Tinian 1944*, CAM 152: *Kasserine Pass 1943*, CAM 158: *El Alamein 1942*, CAM 159: *Berlin 1945*, CAM 167: *Moscow 1941*, CAM 181: *Siegfried Line 1944–45*, CAM 184: *Stalingrad 1942*, CAM 186 *Operation Barbarossa* 1941 (3), CAM 189: *Sevastopol 1942*, CAM 196: *Gazala 1942*, CAM 205: *Warsaw 1944*, CAM 215: *Leningrad 1941–44*, CAM 226: *Midway 1942*, CAM 232: *The Bismarck 1941*, CAM 254: *Kharkov 1942*, CAM 265: *Fall Gelb 1940 (2)*, CAM 270: *Operation Market-Garden 1944 (1)*, CAM 272: *Kursk 1943*, CAM 284: *Guadalcanal 1942*, CAM 293: *Downfall 1945*, CAM 300: *Malaya and Singapore 1941–42*, CAM 305: *Kursk 1943*, CAM 313: *The Philippine Sea 1944*, and CAM 319: *Imphal 1944*.

Cut-out artworks previously published in: NVG 224: *Polish Armor of the Blitzkrieg* (p.11), MAA 493: *Hitler's Blitzkrieg Enemies 1940* (p.15), DUE 029: *Hurricane I vs Bf 110* (p.19), ELI 132: *German Commanders of World War II (2)* (p.23), MAA 326: *The German Army 1939–45 (3)* (p.27), WAR 142: *Blue Division Soldier 1941–45* (p.31), MAA 365: *World War II German Battle Insignia* (p.35), MAA 246: *The Romanian Army of World War II* (p.39), COM 119: *Nakajima B5N 'Kate' and B6N 'Jill' Units* (p.43), WAR 66: *British Infantryman in the Far East 1941–45* (p.47), DUE 4: *Panther vs T-34* (p.51), WAR 149: *Afrikakorps Soldier 1941–43* (p.55), COM 20: *TBD Devastator Units of the US Navy* (p.59), ELI 222: *World War II US Marine Infantry Regiments* (p.63), MAA 508: *World War II Croatian Legionaries* (p.67), MAA 368: *The British Army 1939–45 (2)* (p.71), NVG 113: *M3 Lee/Grant Medium Tank 1941–45* (p.75), MAA 216: *The Red Army of the Great Patriotic War 1941–45* (pp.79 and 127), MAA 486: *The New Zealand Expeditionary Force in World War II* (p.83), MAA 375: *The British Army 1939–45 (3)* (p.87), ELI 219: *D-Day Beach Assault Troops* (p.91), WAR 95: *Japanese Infantryman 1937–45* (p 95), DUE 62: *F6F Hellcat vs A6M Zero-sen* (p.99), MAA 117: *The Polish Army 1939–45* (p.103), WAR 26: *US Paratrooper 1941–45* (p.107), ELI 100: *World War II Axis Booby Traps and Sabotage Tactics* (p.111), ELI 11: *Ardennes 1944 Peiper & Skorzeny* (p.115), ELI 92: *World War II Medal of Honor Recipients (1)* (p.119), and ACE 119: *F6F Hellcat Aces of VF-9* (p.123).

A catalogue record for this book is available from the British Library.

Print ISBN: 978 1 4728 3555 0 – ePub: 978 1 4728 3554 3
ePDF: 978 1 4728 3553 6 – XML: 978 1 4728 3556 7

Index by Mark Swift
Originated by PDQ Digital Media Solutions, Bungay, UK
Printed and bound in India by Replika Press Private Ltd.

23 24 25 26 27   10 9 8 7 6 5 4

Image acknowledgements

Front cover artwork by Steve Noon and back cover artwork by Peter Dennis, all © Osprey Publishing Ltd.

Acknowledgements

Special thanks to Kieran Whitworth of the Imperial War Museums for his idea and support of this book.

The Woodland Trust

Osprey Publishing supports the Woodland Trust, the UK's leading woodland conservation charity.

www.ospreypublishing.com

To find out more about our authors and books visit our website. Here you will find extracts, author interviews, details of forthcoming events and the option to sign-up for our newsletter.

CONTENTS

CHRONOLOGY

1939
1 Sept.	Germany invades Poland.
3 Sept.	Britain and France declare war on Germany.

1940
9 Apr.	Germany invades Denmark and Norway.
10 May	Germany invades France and Low Countries.
10–28 May	Battle of Belgium
26 May–4 June	Allied troops withdraw from Dunkirk.
22 June	France surrenders.
3–5 July	Battle of Mers-el-Kebir.
10 July–31 Oct.	Battle of Britain.
28 Oct.	Italy invades Greece.

1941
28 Mar.	Battle of Cape Matapan.
6 Apr.	Germany invades Greece and Yugoslavia.
20 May	German airborne invasion of Crete.
27 May	*Bismarck* sunk by the British.
22 June–5 Dec.	Operation *Barbarossa*, Axis invasion of Soviet Union.
19 Sept.–27 Jan 1944	Siege of Leningrad.
2 Oct.–7 Jan. 1942	Battle of Moscow.

30 Oct.–4 July 1942	Siege of Sevastopol.
7 Dec.	Japan attacks Pearl Harbor.
8 Dec.	Siege of Tobruk raised.
8 Dec.–31 Jan 1942	Malayan Campaign fought.
11 Dec.	Germany declares war on the US.
14 Dec.	Japanese start invasion of Burma.
17 Dec.	First Battle of Sirte.

1942
27 Feb.	Naval Battle of Java Sea.
22 Mar.	Second Battle of Sirte.
5–8 May	Battle of the Coral Sea.
12–28 May	Second Battle of Kharkov.
26 May–21 June	Battle of Gazala.
4–7 June	Battle of Midway.
1–27 July	First Battle of El Alamein.
July–Feb 1943	Battle of Guadalcanal.
8–9 Aug.	Naval Battle of Savo Island.
23 Aug.–2 Feb. 1943	Battle of Stalingrad.
23 Oct.–11 Nov.	Second Battle of El Alamein.
8 Nov.	Operation *Torch*, Anglo-American invasion of Vichy French North Africa.
12–15 Nov.	Naval Battle of Guadalcanal.
17 Nov–9 May 1943	Battle for Tunisia.

1943

14–22 Feb.	Battle of Kasserine Pass, Tunisia.
2–4 Mar.	Battle of the Bismarck Sea.
10 July	Operation *Husky*, Allied invasion of Sicily.
12 July–23 Aug.	Battle of Kursk.
12 July	Germans lose Prokhorovka tank battle.
20 Nov.	American forces invade Makin and Tarawa.

1944

17 Jan.–18 May	Battle of Monte Cassino.
31 Jan.	Americans invade Marshall Islands.
8 Mar.–3 July	Battle of Imphal.
6 June	D-Day: the Normandy landings.
10 June	Soviets start offensive against Finland.
15 June–9 July	Battle of Saipan.
19–20 June	Battle of the Philippine Sea.
19–30 June	Battle for Cherbourg, France.
23 June–29 Aug.	Soviet *Bagration* offensive.
21 July	Americans invade Guam.
1 Aug.–2 Oct.	The Warsaw Uprising.
15 Aug.	Operation *Dragoon*, Allied invasion of southern France.
Aug.	Romania, Bulgaria and Finland declare war on Germany.

17–25 Sept.	Allied Operation *Market-Garden*.
19 Sept.–16 Dec.	Battle of Hürtgen Forest.
21 Oct.	Fall of Aachen, Germany: Siegfried Line penetrated.
23–26 Oct.	Naval Battle of Leyte Gulf.
4 Nov.	Greece completely liberated.
16 Dec.–25 Jan. 1945	Battle of the Bulge.

1945

19 Feb.–26 Mar.	Battle of Iwo Jima.
1 Apr.–22 June	Battle of Okinawa.
16 Apr.–2 May	Battle of Berlin.
28 Apr.	Mussolini captured and executed by partisans.
30 Apr.	Hitler commits suicide.
2 May	Berlin garrison and German forces in Italy surrender, formal end to war in the Mediterranean.
7 Aug.	Atomic bomb dropped on Hiroshima.
8 Aug.	Soviet Union declares war on Japan.
9 Aug.	Atomic bomb dropped on Nagasaki.
14 Aug.	Unconditional surrender of Japanese forces.
15 Aug.	VJ-Day; all offensive action against Japan ends.

THE INVASION OF POLAND

1 September–6 October 1939

The 1939 Polish Campaign marked the beginning of World War II, and witnessed the first combination of the new technologies of armoured vehicles, combat aircraft and radio communications to create a devastating new form of high-speed, combined-arms warfare.

In 1939, the Wehrmacht enjoyed numerous advantages over the Polish Army in both quality and quantity. Between 1935 and 1939, Germany's defence expenditure was 30 times greater than that of Poland during the same period. Moreover, the German Army was more than three times the size of the Polish.

The Wehrmacht committed its best divisions to the campaign. For the invasion of Poland, Army Group North had a total of 630,000 personnel earmarked, with a further 886,000 allocated to the more powerful Army Group South. Many Polish formations were only partially mobilized, while German units were on war footing at the outset of the campaign.

LEFT The Junkers Ju 87B Stuka is the icon of blitzkrieg warfare. Here, two Stukas are attacked by a Polish P.11c fighter, September 1939. (Howard Gerrard © Osprey Publishing)

The first act of the invasion began around 4.00am on 1 September when the German battleship *Schleswig-Holstein* slipped its moorings in Danzig and began a bombardment of the neighbouring Polish transit base on Westerplatte. This marked the beginning of the phase known as the Battle of the Border.

A few hours later, Warsaw was struck by the first air raids, and Polish airfields were attacked, with the Luftwaffe seeking to gain air supremacy. After a few days, the Luftwaffe would begin to shift more of its operations to missions supporting the ground forces, bombing road and rail junctions and Polish troop concentrations – as well as civilian targets. Although numerically inferior, the Polish Air Force would remain active until the second week of the invasion, continuing to inflict losses on the Luftwaffe.

The German land campaign comprised attacks from three separate directions. On 1 September, Army Group North, under Colonel-General Fedor von Bock, began its attack into northern Poland. The German Fourth Army, under Lieutenant-General Günther von Kluge, crossed the border and secured the Pomeranian Corridor in north-western Poland, forcing the Polish Army Pomorze into a fighting withdrawal southward to more defensible positions. By 3 September, von Kluge's forces had crossed the Vistula River.

Meanwhile, the German Third Army in East Prussia (also under Army Group North command) attacked southwards towards Warsaw. Two corps began the assault, which soon became entangled in the Mlawa fortification line. After a few days, the Polish defences collapsed. The Third Army linked up with von Kluge's Fourth Army at the Vistula on 3 September.

The driving force in the Wehrmacht's assault on Poland was Colonel-General Gerd von Rundstedt's Army Group South, especially its two northern elements, the Eighth and Tenth Armies in Silesia. These formations were to crash through the opposing Army Lodz and Army Krakow, cross the Warta River, envelope the Polish forces along the western frontier and drive on Warsaw from the south. Also in the south, a joint German–Slovak force pushed across the border into Poland from northern Slovakia.

Polish forces began to retreat across all the fronts, adopting deeper defensive positions. Army Groups North and South linked up at Lodz in central Poland on 6 September, trapping the remaining Polish forces up against the border with Germany. Gradually, the Polish Army was forced into several isolated pockets that were gradually eliminated by overwhelming German firepower.

By 7 September, the Polish forces defending Warsaw had fallen back to a line running parallel with the Vistula River. The following day, German armoured units reached the outskirts of Warsaw, which entered a state of siege and was repeatedly bombed. Any form of coordinated Polish resistance now began to fragment into piecemeal opposition. The major cities of Lodz and Poznan were also now being cut off by German encirclement.

On 9 September, the Polish Army managed to launch a counter-offensive near the Bzura River, west of Warsaw, striking the flank of the advancing German Eighth Army. This evolved into the largest battle of the invasion of Poland, extending over ten days. However, the German counter-attack, combined with overwhelming air power, managed to outflank the Polish forces, and overran all of western Poland. This proved to be the decisive turning point of the invasion. The Luftwaffe managed to destroy the bridges across the Bzura, leaving Polish forces trapped out in the open, and they were easily picked off.

By 12 September, all of Polish territory west of the Vistula River was under German control, save for besieged Warsaw. A general Polish retreat was ordered to the south-east, to the hills bordering Romania and the Soviet Union, in an effort to buy time.

Stalin's Red Army invaded eastern Poland on 17 September, opening a second front. Germany had entered into the Ribbentrop–Molotov pact with the Soviet Union a week before the start of the invasion, and while the two nations' Marxist and Nazi ideologies seemed diametrically opposed, their shared interests of restoring the pre-1919 territorial boundaries now converged. The Red Army was organized into two fronts and deployed 25 rifle divisions, 16 cavalry divisions and 12 tank brigades, with a total strength of 466,516 troops. Polish defences had been stripped bare in the east, and the force ratio was ludicrously one-sided: roughly one Polish battalion per Soviet corps.

The final battle of the invasion took place at Kock between 2 and 5 October 1939. Here, a large Polish force located between the Bug and Vistula rivers was destroyed by the German Tenth Army.

Although Poland never formally surrendered, by 6 October it was under complete German and Soviet control. Polish casualties amounted to about 66,300 dead, 133,700 wounded, 587,000 prisoners captured by Germany and over 100,000 by the Soviet Union.

For the German Army, the invasion was a necessary test of men and machines. It had still not perfected its novel tactics, and German casualties (16,000 dead and 32,000 wounded) were relatively heavy for such a short campaign. The invasion of Poland uncovered the shortcomings in German training and doctrine, and made it possible for the Wehrmacht to perfect blitzkrieg prior to its greatest challenge: the assault on France and the Low Countries in 1940.

RIGHT A single-turret 7TP (7-Tonne Polish) light tank, the most capable tank in Poland's inventory. (Henry Morshead © Osprey Publishing)

THE BATTLE OF BELGIUM

10–28 May 1940

The Battle of Belgium formed part of the greater Battle of France. It took place over 18 days in May 1940, and included the first tank battle of the war (and the largest to that date) – the Battle of Hannut – as well as the Battle of Fort Eben Emael, which was the first strategic airborne operation using paratroopers ever attempted.

On 27 September 1939, as the invasion of Poland was drawing to a close, Adolf Hitler met with the commanders-in-chief of the three Wehrmacht services and announced his intention to invade France through 'Belgium and the Dutch appendix of Maastricht'. To achieve this, in little more than three weeks the Army High Command developed *Fall Gelb* (*Case Yellow*). It called for an offensive directly through Belgium and southern Holland, with the initial assaults swinging around the north and south sides of the fortress-ringed city of Liège before driving to the coast. Lieutenant-

LEFT The French 11th Mounted Dragoon Regiment and a battery of four 25mm anti-tank guns defend Jandrain, 13 May 1940. (Peter Dennis © Osprey Publishing)

General Günther von Kluge's Fourth Army, followed by Twelfth Army, was to bypass Liège to the south and then merge with General Walter von Reichenau's Sixth Army in central Belgium for the drive to the Channel coast.

The planning for *Fall Gelb* was subsequently modified to include the subjugation of the Netherlands, and also to switch the main weight of the German assault to the south wing of the offensive. Army Group A became the main striking force, with four armies totalling 45 divisions and 75 per cent of the Wehrmacht's mechanized forces: its armoured formations were to achieve a major breakthrough between Sedan in France, and Dinant in Belgium. Von Reichenau's Sixth Army was now to cross the Maas River and drive into Belgium with five infantry corps, in a move designed to convince the Allied command that it was the main thrust (a ruse known as the 'Matador's Cloak'). At the same time, the Fallschirmjäger (paratrooper) element of the Luftwaffe's 7th Air Division would seize the Maas and Rhine bridges, and neutralize Fort Eben Emael, which guarded the bridges entering northern Belgium.

The Allies had drawn up the Dyle Plan for helping Belgium, whereby the best Allied forces, including the British Expeditionary Force and the French First Army, would advance to the Dyle River in the event of a German invasion. If the Allies 'took the German bait', their best mobile forces would be prevented from being able to respond to Army Group A's panzers approaching Sedan through the thickly forested hills of the Ardennes.

The Belgian Army was relatively strong, and defensively orientated. Mobilized on 26 August 1939, its size had swollen to 22 divisions. Although manpower had reached 600,000 troops by May 1940, over half of these were still in training. The Belgian defensive plan relied heavily on the Albert Canal fortifications, which were some of the most modern defensive positions in Europe. However, once the invasion began, they proved to be virtually useless.

On 10 May, the Luftwaffe launched its glider assault to capture the bridges spanning the Albert Canal west of Maastricht and Fort Eben Emael and its 1,200-strong garrison. At the same time, the Luftwaffe bomber arm quickly devastated many Belgian airfields and communication centres, and its fighters achieved complete aerial supremacy over central Belgium.

The Allies enacted the Dyle Plan as soon as the invasion began. Any delay to the German onslaught was beneficial as far as they were concerned. The French First Army was to 'plug' the unfortified Gembloux Gap, initially with Prioux's mechanized Cavalry Corps; alerted at 7.45am on 10 May, Prioux's armoured cars, tanks, lorried infantry and towed artillery left Valenciennes and Maubeuge, and began crossing the Belgian border four hours later, followed that evening by three motorized infantry divisions. The Matador's Cape was working to perfection, with the French fully committing the best of the armies to Belgium between 10 and 12 May. On the 12th, the French First Army arrived at Gembloux, between Wavre and Namur.

The Belgian Air Force and the Royal Air Force (RAF) attempted to bomb the Albert Canal bridges and positions that the Germans had captured intact and were holding on 11 May. However, faced with encirclement, the Belgian infantry units began to withdraw from the Albert Canal's west bank. The gateways into central Belgium were now opened for the German panzers.

General Erich Hoepner's XVI Army Corps (motorized) drove deep into central Belgium, advancing in strength against the French mechanized cavalry, which was being constantly watched by roving German observation aircraft. Hoepner's two panzer divisions drove towards Hannut in battle array. The swift panzer advance resulted in the first great tank battle of the war, a three-day-long, head-on clash of modern armoured fighting vehicles in which German doctrine, mobility, flexibility, command and communications overcame superior French armour and armament.

At the same time, Army Group A launched the main phase of *Fall Gelb*, breaking through the defences at Sedan on 15 May, and advancing towards the English Channel. Its troops reached the Channel on 19 May, encircling the rapidly retreating Allied armies. By 21 May, German forces had trapped the British Expeditionary Force (BEF), the remnants of the Belgian Army, and the French armies along the northern coast of France. Slowly, the Allied pockets were reduced, and evacuation across the Channel became the only option for the commander of the BEF, General Viscount Gort.

Seperated from the BEF, physically spent and without further reserves, and with no means of following the Allies to Dunkirk, King Léopold of Belgium realized that his army's situation was now hopeless. After 17 days of hard fighting, the Belgian surrender came into effect at 5.00am on 28 May. Major-General Jules Derousseaux, representing King Léopold,

signed the formal surrender document. Belgian casualties amounted to around 6,000 killed and 15,850 wounded, with many more captured and imprisoned until the end of the war.

Belgium was now an occupied country, and would remain so until 1944. To paraphrase Winston Churchill, 'the Battle of Belgium was over. The Battle of Dunkirk was about to begin': over 112,000 British and French troops would be evacuated from the beaches and harbour of Dunkirk in France between 26 May and 4 June 1940 during Operation *Dynamo*.

RIGHT A Belgian chief warrant officer, Liège Fortress Regiment at Eben Emael, 10 May 1940. (Johnny Shumate © Osprey Publishing)

THE BATTLE OF BRITAIN

10 July–31 October 1940

The epic clash of air forces over southern England during the late summer and autumn of 1940 – known as the Battle of Britain – was, in fact, both the goal and the culmination of Adolf Hitler's *Westfeldzug* (Western Campaign), which began on 10 May 1940 with the invasion of the Low Countries and France. It was one of the decisive battles of World War II, and saw the RAF defeat a German attempt to gain air superiority over southern England. The battle was also the first major defeat to be suffered by the Germans during the war.

The Wehrmacht's strategic planning for defeating Britain in 1940 lay in the hope of an effective U-boat blockade and a strategic air offensive against British ports, armaments industries, and oil refinery and storage facilities. However, the German Navy (Kriegsmarine), which saw large numbers of its U-boats sunk during the opening phase of the Battle of the Atlantic and was struggling to train up replacement crews,

had few ocean-going U-boats available. In the short term, therefore, only the newest of Germany's military services – the Luftwaffe – could effectively carry the war to the British.

On 22 November 1939, the Luftwaffe intelligence office produced a proposal for the 'Conduct of Air Warfare against Britain', a conceptual strategic air offensive plan. A week later, Hitler issued Führer Directive No. 9, 'Conduct of the War against the Economy of the Enemy', which authorized the Luftwaffe to begin bombing British ports, depots, oil and food storage, and industrial plants once suitable airfields were captured in northern France, Belgium and Holland. By May the following year, with Holland and Belgium having fallen and France on the verge of capitulation, Hitler issued Führer Directive No. 13, authorizing the Luftwaffe 'to attack the English homeland in the fullest manner, as soon as sufficient forces are available … in accordance with principles laid down in Directive No. 9'. On 30 June, Luftwaffe chief Hermann Göring issued orders implementing this directive to his 2nd, 3rd and 5th Air Fleets.

The first phase of the Battle of Britain was termed the *Kanalkampf* (Channel Battle), and took place between 2 July and 11 August 1940. The actions followed the strategic intent laid down in Hitler's Führer Directive No. 9. During this phase, the first plans were formed for an invasion of the British Isles, Operation *Seelöwe* (*Sealion*), which was later abandoned.

Towards the end of July 1940, German tactical planning shifted the focus of air operations away from targeting infrastructure to an offensive counter-air campaign against the RAF. On 1 August, Hitler's Führer Directive No. 17 ordered the Luftwaffe to 'overpower the English air force with all the forces at its command, in the shortest possible time… in order to establish [air superiority] for the final conquest of England.' This would be known as Operation *Adlerangriff* (*Eagle Attack*). The Luftwaffe would now be directed against RAF installations and British aviation industries, with Royal Navy installations as secondary targets.

Adlerangriff was launched on 12 August 1940, with preliminary bombardments targeting six RAF radar stations and three coastal fighter airfields. The following day, known as *Adlertag* (*Eagle Day*), the Luftwaffe's counter-air campaign against the RAF officially began. The first phase of the operations, between 12 and 18 August, saw attacks launched against the RAF in general, with secondary attacks against naval facilities and ports.

Adlerangriff's second phase, between 24 August and 6 September 1940, saw attacks concentrated against RAF Fighter Command's No. 11 Group sector stations and fighter airfields in south-east England. Despite Göring's promises to Hitler of a swift victory, and the heavy damage and casualties inflicted on the RAF, these first phases of *Eagle Attack* failed to make a significant impression on Fighter Command's ability to defend Britain's air space.

The 'Hardest Day' took place on 18 August 1940. The Luftwaffe's all-out effort to destroy Fighter Command gave rise to some of the largest air battles ever seen to that point. Both sides suffered heavy losses, with Luftwaffe losses in the air double those of the British. However, the RAF lost many planes to ground attack. The combined Luftwaffe and RAF losses on this day would remain unsurpassed for the remainder of the Battle of Britain.

From late August, a further tactical shift took place. Both the Luftwaffe and RAF, at first unintentionally it appears, became embroiled in tit-for-tat bombing raids against London and Berlin. However, both sides quickly realized the potential for targeting civilians directly in the campaign, and on 5 September the Luftwaffe's first intentional bombing of London took place. The Luftwaffe's High Command now planned to use its attacks against London (known as the Blitz) in the hope of drawing RAF Fighter Command into battle: this comprised the third phase of Operation *Adlerangriff,* between 7 and 30 September 1940. During this period, London was systematically bombed by the Luftwaffe night and day.

The 15th of September 1940 is widely regarded as the climax to the Battle of Britain, and is now commemorated as Battle of Britain Day in the UK. On that day, a massive Luftwaffe attack against London took place. Over 1,100 aircraft struck the British capital, in a clash that lasted from morning until dusk. Losses to German bombers were particularly heavy.

On 17 September, with air superiority still not achieved, Hitler postponed Operation *Seelöwe* indefinitely, essentially cancelling the proposed invasion of Great Britain, and signalling the Luftwaffe's defeat. Throughout the campaign, the Luftwaffe had continually underestimated the capability and importance of British radar systems.

The Luftwaffe's last major daylight attack on London took place on 30 September, followed on 29 October by its final major daylight bombing mission. The Blitz continued in the form of night bombing raids (in order to avoid RAF fighters), and included other major British cities beyond London. However, once again the Luftwaffe raids failed to weaken civilian morale, and did not inflict lasting damage on Britain's industrial output, a result chiefly of the lack of a coherent, methodical German tactical approach to crippling the British wartime economy.

RIGHT This Hurricane Mk I was flown by Pilot Officer McGrath of No. 601 Sqn during the Battle of Britain. (Jim Laurier © Osprey Publishing)

THE SINKING OF THE *BISMARCK*

27 May 1941

Launched in February 1939 and commissioned on 24 August 1940, the *Bismarck* combined an impressive and integrated armament with an excellent design, making her a hugely powerful warship. Between August 1940 and May 1941, 'the unsinkable ship' remained one of the most serious threats that Britain faced – one that could single-handedly sever its vital convoy lifelines and bring about the defeat of the island nation – even though she was yet to make her maiden voyage.

Great Britain depended on merchant shipping in order to satisfy its food and raw material needs, and protecting the lifeline across the Atlantic was one of the nation's, and the Royal Navy's, highest priorities during World War II. Germany's U-boats sank hundreds of thousands of tons of Allied shipping every month. However, in 1941 Grand Admiral Erich Raeder, commander of the Kriegsmarine, was aware that he still lacked sufficient U-boats to have a decisive effect, and that he needed to use all the assets at his disposal, including the *Bismarck*.

LEFT The final destruction of the *Bismarck* by HMS *Dorsetshire*, 9.45am, 27 May 1941. (Paul Wright © Osprey Publishing)

The Germans planned to unleash the *Bismarck* in May 1941. Her maiden voyage was to be a sortie deep into the North Atlantic against Allied shipping, codenamed Operation *Rheinübung*, in the company of the heavy cruiser *Prinz Eugen*. The *Bismarck* was considered fast enough to slip past the British warships blocking her path into the Atlantic, and, if it came to a fight, her guns were more than a match for any single battleship that the Royal Navy could send against her. *Rheinübung* came on the coat tails of Operation *Berlin*, a highly successful sortie by the German ships *Scharnhorst* and *Gneisenau* in early 1941; however, the latter two had suffered damage, and were under repair in Brest in May 1941.

What ensued was a giant maritime game of cat and mouse. Finding a single ship in the vast expanse of the North Atlantic is a difficult task even today, but in 1941 it was that much harder as the weather conditions were poor, radar was in its infancy, and, for a crucial 24 hours, the British had no real idea where to look.

Operation *Rheinübung* began on Sunday 18 May 1941, 13 days after Hitler had proudly inspected the *Bismarck*, accompanied by Admiral Günther Lütjens (who would command *Rheinübung*), at Gotenhafen (Gdynia) on the Baltic. The *Bismarck* and *Prinz Eugen* proceeded to sea, and rendezvoused with three destroyers off the island of Rügen.

On 20 May, the German ships began a four-hour transit of the Great Belt in Danish waters, and at 1.00pm that day the *Bismarck* was sighted in the Kattegat by the Swedish cruiser *Gotland*, which called it in during a routine report. Sources in the Swedish Government relayed this information to the British Admiralty.

On Wednesday 21 May, the German group of ships entered the Korsfjord, near Bergen in Norway, and anchored in the Grimstadfjord. There, the *Bismarck* was once again spotted, this time by a Coastal Command reconnaissance plane. That evening, at 8.00pm, the German group left the Korsfjord, and headed out to sea on a northerly course for the Atlantic shipping lanes.

Meanwhile, the Admiralty had ordered HMS *Hood* and HMS *Prince of Wales*, accompanied by a destroyer escort, to head for the Denmark Strait, where the cruisers HMS *Norfolk* and HMS *Suffolk* were on patrol.

The destroyers separated from the German group of ships on Thursday 22 May, and returned to the Korsfjord, while the *Bismarck* and *Prinz Eugen* altered course for the Denmark Strait. Alerted to the departure of the German vessels, Admiral

Sir John Tovey sailed with HMS *King George V*, HMS *Victorious* and escort vessels from Scapa Flow in the Orkneys.

On Friday 23 May at 7.22pm, HMS *Suffolk* sighted the *Bismarck*, and reported her position. An hour later, the *Bismarck* sighted HMS *Norfolk*, and engaged her, without scoring a hit. The two British cruisers evaded the *Bismarck* and *Prinz Eugen*, then shadowed them through the night.

Things came to a head on Saturday 24 May, in the Battle of the Denmark Strait. At just after 5.30am that morning, HMS *Hood* and *Prince of Wales* were spotted by the German vessels at a range of 17 miles, and 20 minutes later the two sides began a gunnery duel. At 6.00am, *Hood* was hit by a salvo from the *Bismarck*, which ignited one of her magazines. The resultant explosion broke her in two and she sank, taking with her all but three of her 1,417 crew. The *Prince of Wales* was also hit and retired from the battle shortly after. The *Bismarck* had not escaped unharmed, however, with the crew reporting an oil leak. Just before 1.00pm, she headed south for repairs in the direction of St Nazaire, still shadowed by the British cruisers. Just after 6.00pm, the undamaged *Prinz Eugen* separated from the *Bismarck* to continue the raiding mission, leaving her to attempt to draw off the pursuers.

At 12.15am on Sunday 25 May, the *Bismarck* was attacked by Swordfish aircraft from HMS *Victorious*; one torpedo hit her amidships, but no significant damage was caused. The *Bismarck* managed to evade her pursuers at 3.00am, but Admiral Lütjens broke radio silence to report back to Grand Admiral Raeder. The British intercepted the lengthy transmission, and managed to calculate the *Bismarck*'s approximate position.

The following day, the *Bismarck* was spotted by a Catalina flying boat, and HMS *Sheffield* managed to locate her, shadowing her passage. At 9.00pm, the *Bismarck* was attacked by Swordfish from HMS *Ark Royal*. She was hit twice, and her rudder jammed. With her speed down to 7 knots, she was dead in the water.

Early on Tuesday 27 May, the *Bismarck* was sighted by HMS *Rodney* and *King George V*. *Rodney* opened fire at 8.47am, followed a minute later by *King George V*. *Bismarck* returned fire, aiming at *Rodney*. After ten minutes a hit disabled the *Bismarck*'s forward gunnery director, which made it far more difficult for her to aim her guns with any real accuracy. Over the next 30 minutes the *Bismarck* was hit repeatedly, losing the use of her after gunnery director, and all of her four turrets. She became a blazing wreck, almost incapable of defending herself.

The British battleships closed the range, and kept firing: the majority of their shells hit their target. The *Bismarck* was still floating, but she was listing slightly to port owing to flooding from several waterline hits, and her superstructure forward of her after turrets was ablaze.

The firing would continue for 30 more minutes, by which time it was clear that the *Bismarck* would not be sunk by gunnery alone. At that point Tovey ordered his two battleships to break off the action, and sent in the cruiser *Dorsetshire* to finish off the *Bismarck* with her torpedoes. She finally sank at 10.40am.

RIGHT Grand Admiral Erich Raeder in admirals' full dress service uniform, 1939. (Malcolm McGregor © Osprey Publishing)

OPERATION *BARBAROSSA*

22 June–5 December 1941

Nazi Germany's invasion of the Soviet Union on 22 June 1941, Operation *Barbarossa*, has no equal in military history. By nearly any measure – numbers of combatants involved, physical scope, violence and ruination – the operation was immense. *Barbarossa* witnessed the assembly of the largest invasion force in the history of warfare, comprising 3.5 million Axis troops, and was launched across a 2,900km front.

Planning for *Barbarossa* had begun back in December 1940 with Hitler's Führer Directive No. 21. The overarching strategic aims were to conquer the western Soviet Union, subjugate its Slavic populations, and create 'living space' for ethnic Germans.

A German victory in *Barbarossa* was universally defined as destruction of the Red Army west of the Dvina and Dnepr rivers – and a key German failure was to not set clear

objectives for operations beyond this. Due to the enormous size of the Soviet Union, three separate army groups were tasked with achieving this goal.

Army Group North's plan for reaching Leningrad, 500 miles away, would see General Erich Hoepner's 4th Panzer Group punch through the Soviets' frontier defences and make for the Dvina River crossings near Dünaburg, from there aiming towards Opochka. Depending on Leningrad's defences, Hoepner would either advance due north or swing north-east. The Eighteenth Army would clear the Baltic region and be prepared to take the islands off Estonia's coast. The Sixteenth Army had responsibility for securing the boundary with Army Group Centre.

Army Group Centre, under Field Marshal Fedor von Bock, received the mission of destroying Red Army forces in Belorussia. Panzer groups on the flanks represented von Bock's main punch, with infantry armies marching in between. After encircling an initial *Kessel* ('cauldron' – i.e. pocket) at Minsk, Army Group Centre's operational goals were Vitebsk and Orsha (the Dvina–Dnepr Line), to be followed by a three-week logistical pause. The outer wings would then swing wide and meet again to create another pocket at Smolensk.

In Army Group South, the German Army's senior officer, Field Marshal Gerd von Rundstedt, commanded 46 and a half divisions along a front of more than 800 miles. With the largest operational area of any army group, yet only one panzer group, his men had four difficult tasks: destroying Red Army units to their front; capturing the Ukrainian capital of Kiev and the Dnepr River crossings; seizing the Donets Basin; and opening the route to the Caucasus oil region.

Barbarossa began with brutal border battles, followed by stunning achievements by the Wehrmacht. By mid-July 1941, panzer groups were within striking distance of Leningrad, Smolensk and Kiev. Soviet counter-attacks following pre-war plans all failed because of a pattern of poor command and control, inexperience, and German operational and tactical acumen. However, the Red Army then initiated a second wave of countermoves, most notably those bearing Marshal Semyon Timoshenko's name, along the Moscow axis. Although many forces earmarked for operational purposes were squandered on tactical missions, these attacks signalled that the Soviets would not give up the Dvina–Dnepr Line without a fight.

Von Bock's Army Group Centre trapped 300,000 Red Army soldiers at Minsk, and then in late July 1941 closed a similarly large but more strategically significant *Kessel* at Smolensk. Von Rundstedt's Army Group South surrounded two Soviet armies on 8 August and captured 100,000 men in the Uman pocket, before pushing on to reach the Dnepr River.

Operational triumph eluded Army Group North, however. Following the capture of Novgorod, Field Marshal Wilhelm Ritter von Leeb ordered a costly and time-consuming assault across the upper Luga River. Although Army Group North eventually cut off Leningrad, the USSR's second city, from overland communication, von Leeb's attack essentially halted at this point.

By the end of July 1941, *Barbarossa* had begun to stall, as the Führer argued with his generals over the prosecution of its second phase. While he issued a series of contradictory Führer Directives, commanders on the ground fought *Barbarossa* as they saw fit. The generals renewed calls to assault Moscow, while the dictator wanted action on the flanks.

The campaign moved forward, albeit rudderless, until Hitler resolved the matter in late August. Never in favour of a direct attack on Moscow, Hitler had strategic reasons for taking decisive action on *Barbarossa*'s wings. Success at either extreme could possibly bring Turkey into the war or motivate Finland to redouble its efforts. Germany needed every last resource of the Ukraine. Equally, the German Army could not ignore the mass of troops, among the Red Army's best, sitting on the boundary between Army Groups Centre and South. A decision to push towards Kiev was made, and German forces moved south quickly to capture the city.

Stalin, focused on Moscow and distracted by Luftwaffe bombing of the capital, missed the move. Colonel-General Paul von Kleist's Panzer Group, held up on the Irpen River (thus giving the Soviets greater opportunity to evacuate Ukrainian industry), sought the line of least resistance on his right, and thereby created a huge salient. These two armoured jaws slamming shut at Lochvitsa represented the zenith of German operational art, but victory at Kiev was soon offset by superior Soviet force generation.

During the second half of September, the German generals demonstrated how fast they could move when they wanted to by reorienting two and a half panzer groups plus numerous infantry formations from the Leningrad and Kiev areas to the Moscow axis. Von Bock's last great victory came at Viazma–Bryansk. He was then abruptly slowed, by weather (first in the form of mud and later by sub-zero cold) combined with the 'four horsemen' of Nazi strategic overstretch: troop exhaustion, personnel and materiel attrition, overstretched logistics, and the continuing inability to settle on attainable objectives.

Barbarossa was brought to a close on 5 December, as Hitler ordered the Wehrmacht to assume a defensive stance on the whole front. Despite the huge losses inflicted on the Red Army, *Barbarossa* had failed to achieve a Soviet capitulation. Moreover, the Soviet winter counter-offensive now underway would eliminate the German threat to Moscow.

RIGHT A junior officer from Panzer-Regiment 39, Smolensk, July 1942. (Stephen Andrew © Osprey Publishing)

THE SIEGE OF LENINGRAD
8 September 1941–27 January 1944

The Siege of Leningrad, the Soviet Union's second largest city, was one of the longest and most destructive sieges in the history of warfare. This lengthy blockade was undertaken by Army Group North, the Spanish Blue Division and the Finnish Army between 1941 and 1944, and resulted in the deaths of an estimated 700,000 civilians.

Leningrad was a vital city in the Soviet Union. By 1940, it had a population of 2.54 million, making it the fourth largest city in Europe. Its factories produced about 10 per cent of the Soviet Union's entire industrial output, including much of its high-quality steel and the new KV-1 heavy tank.

As war in Europe approached, Stalin resolved to safeguard Leningrad by pushing the Soviet Union's vulnerable border areas back as far as possible from the city. After Finland refused to sell part of the Karelian Isthmus adjoining the Leningrad Military District, the Red Army seized the land by

LEFT The 'Five-Kopeck' bridgehead over the Neva River was held by the Soviets for 222 days at a cost of about 30,000 dead. (Peter Dennis © Osprey Publishing)

force between November 1939 and March 1940. Next, Stalin moved against the pro-German Baltic republics, and in June 1940, Soviet troops marched into Latvia, Lithuania and Estonia. After this, Stalin moved three armies with 440,000 troops into the former Baltic States in an effort to secure Leningrad against any threats from the west.

Leningrad was not identified as a major target in the planning for Operation *Barbarossa*. However, Hitler was adamant that it should receive equal priority with Moscow and Kiev on the axes of advance. It lay in the path of Army Group North, led by Field Marshal Ritter von Leeb, which consisted of the Sixteenth and Eighteenth Armies and General Erich Hoepner's 4th Panzer Group, totalling 475,000 troops in 28 divisions.

In the opening days of *Barbarossa*, Leningrad's ability to defend itself was seriously compromised. The Soviet forces in the Baltic States were badly defeated in the first 18 days, with most of their tanks and aircraft lost. Some 30,000 civilian volunteers in Leningrad were employed to help build defensive fieldwork on the approaches to the city, and

160,000 recruits were organized into eight people's militia divisions in July. These divisions fought a successful delay on the Luga River that stopped Army Group North's headlong advance towards Leningrad for nearly a month. By the time the Germans finally overwhelmed the Luga Line on 16 August, Leningrad's defenders had built a series of dense fortified lines on the south-west approaches to the city.

However, the German advance shifted eastwards, severing the Leningrad–Moscow rail line at Chudovo on 20 August. With Soviet forces in retreat, von Leeb dispatched XXXIX Army Corps to encircle Leningrad from the south-east while massing the rest of Army Group North for a direct assault on the city.

By 2 September 1941, Finnish forces had advanced to the 1939 borders between Finland and the Soviet Union. On 4 September, German artillery began shelling Leningrad, and four days later the city was entirely surrounded by Army Group North. The German encirclement trapped four armies – the 8th, 23rd, 42nd and 55th – inside the city and the nearby Oranienbaum salient, with a total of 20 divisions and over 300,000 troops. There were about 30 days' food reserves on hand in the city, but this was further reduced when the Luftwaffe bombed the Badaev food warehouses on 8 September.

General Georgy Zhukov, newly appointed commander of the Leningrad Front, arrived on 9 September as General Georg-Hans Reinhardt's XXXXI Army Corps began to assault the outer defences of the city. On 16 September, the German XXXVIII Army Corps reached the Gulf of Finland, and the following day, the German 1st Panzer Division managed to approach to within 12km of the city. Zhukov launched a 16-day counter-offensive westward towards Siniavino beginning on 10 September, but this failed to take its objective and casualties were heavy.

On 8 November 1941, in an effort to eliminate the final Soviet links to the encircled city by severing the rail lines that supported the Lake Ladoga barge traffic, the Germans captured Tikhvin. Without this rail junction, the food situation in the city became critical. However, 11 days later a Soviet counter-attack led by 4th Army was launched and it was retaken on 9 December; the Germans, threatened by encirclement, withdrew west.

Meanwhile, on 22 November 1941, the first major Soviet truck convoy managed to cross Lake Ladoga on an ice road and bring some relief to Leningrad. The civilian death toll continued to rise: during the last four months of 1941, German artillery fired over 30,000 rounds into Leningrad, which, in addition to air raids, killed about 4,000 civilians.

On 6 January 1942, the newly established Soviet Volkhov Front launched the Lyuban winter counter-offensive aimed at breaking the blockade. In March, the Soviet 2nd Shock Army was cut off in the Volkhov swamps by German forces.

The Soviets launched a series of failed offensives against the Siniavino Heights over the summer of 1942, but it was not until 18 January 1943 that the Soviet 2nd Shock Army and 67th Army linked up north of Siniavino, establishing a small land corridor into Leningrad. On 15 September 1943, the XXX Guards Rifle Corps finally captured the Heights.

January 1944 witnessed the final moments in the long siege of the city. On 14 January, the 2nd Shock Army began to break out from Oranienbaum, while the 42nd Army attacked out of the city the following day. On 27 January, as the German Eighteenth Army began falling back without orders, the Siege of Leningrad was finally lifted.

Although Army Group North had failed to demolish Leningrad as both a symbol and a centre of Soviet power, in operational terms the siege effectively isolated three Soviet armies for over two years and forced six other armies to conduct repeated costly frontal assaults. Total Soviet military casualties on the Leningrad and Volkhov Fronts during the siege were at least 1.5 million, including 620,000 dead or captured. The siege cost the lives of about 700,000 Soviet civilians and prevented the city's industries from participating fully in the Soviet war effort until mid-1944.

RIGHT Two coats of arms of the Spanish 250th Infantry ('Blue') Division. The division was transferred to the Leningrad front in August 1942, and fought there for the Wehrmacht until October 1943. (Ramiro Bujeiro © Osprey Publishing)

THE BATTLE OF MOSCOW

2 October 1941–7 January 1942

Operation *Typhoon*, the late 1941 German assault in the direction of Moscow, was one of the largest German offensive operations of the entire war. It pitted Army Group Centre's 1.9 million soldiers against the Red Army's 1.25 million men – 40 per cent of its entire strength.

At the end of July, Army Group Centre temporarily moved to the defensive as the German effort switched to Kiev. The Soviets used the respite to rebuild the Western Front in order to protect Moscow. However, instead of husbanding precious reserves, Stalin foolishly squandered them in a series of premature, disastrous offensives in early September 1941.

Hitler considered shifting to a primarily defensive mode along much of the Eastern Front once Kiev and the Ukraine had fallen. Moscow, the capture of which was an ambivalent subject for Hitler, could be taken in the spring of 1942 by a revitalized German Army. However, for once he allowed himself

to be persuaded by a number of German generals, convinced that Moscow would be an easy objective. The Führer Directive No. 35 dated 6 September 1941 ordered a 'decisive operation against [the Western Front], which is conducting unsuccessful offensive operations on Army Group Centre's front. It must be destroyed decisively before the onset of winter', after which Army Group Centre could 'pursue enemy forces along the Moscow axis.' The High Command and Army Group Centre staffs thus developed the operational plan for *Typhoon*.

Typhoon called for two pincer movements by the Germans, one to the north of Moscow against the Kalinin Front by the 3rd and 4th Panzer Groups, and a second one to the south around Bryansk against the Western Front by the 2nd Panzer Group. At the same time, the Fourth Army would advance directly on Moscow from the west.

For the first time in the campaign in the Soviet Union, the Germans enjoyed both quantitative and qualitative superiority; Army Group Centre had an overall 1.5:1 superiority in manpower, 1.7:1 in tanks, 1.8:1 in artillery and 2.1:1 in aircraft. Nevertheless, *Typhoon* was a gamble since the Germans lacked the logistic resources for another protracted offensive and adverse weather would soon impact operational mobility.

The Soviet defensive forces around Moscow consisted of the Western Front (in the centre, under Lieutenant-General Ivan Konev), the Reserve Front (to the north, under Marshal Semyon Budenny) and the Bryansk Front (to the south, under General Andrey Yeremenko). In mid-July 1941, the Soviet leadership had ordered construction of a series of defensive lines around Moscow, consisting of anti-tank ditches, mines and concrete or log bunkers. The outermost line was west of Vyazma, and the inner line was centred on Mozhaisk, on the direct route into Moscow. These lightly manned defences were incomplete at the start of *Typhoon*.

On 30 September, the first phase of *Typhoon* began when General Heinz Guderian's 2nd Panzer Group crashed into the Soviet Bryansk Front, quickly achieving a breakthrough. Bryansk and its Desna River bridges were captured on 6 October. Orel, 100km to the east of Bryansk, also fell to 2nd Panzer Group on 3 October. The Soviet Bryansk Front began to crumble, with the forming Bryansk and Trubchevsk pockets containing the 3rd, 30th and 50th Armies inside.

Meanwhile, on 2 October, the 3rd and 4th Panzer Groups (renamed Panzer Armies three days later) began the main *Typhoon* assault, with the 3rd penetrating the Soviet 30th Army's defences and seizing the bridge over the Dnepr at Kholm and going on to encircle Vyazma. Between 4 and 5 October, von Kluge's 4th Panzer Group crushed the Soviet 33rd and 43rd Armies around Yelnya, sending one corps to encircle Vyazma from the south. Vyazma was fully encircled by the two German armies on 7 October, and elements of four Soviet armies were trapped there.

On 10 October, Second Panzer Army captured Mtsensk. Third Panzer Army seized Rzhev and Kalinin on 13–14 October. With the last resistance in the Vyazma pocket now crushed, the German forces begin reorienting towards Moscow.

The Soviet High Command sensed the danger; on 15 October the government began to evacuate Moscow, and a state of siege was declared. Stalin also recalled Marshal Georgy Zhukov from Leningrad to take command of the overall defence. The Western Front was rebuilt by rushing in reinforcements from other fronts.

On 22 October, Guderian's Second Panzer Army crossed the Zusha River at Mtsensk. The Soviet 29th Army managed to launch an attack on Third Panzer Army's left flank two days later, but its effort was too weak and uncoordinated to cause more than a nuisance. On 27 October, Volokolamsk was captured by the Germans.

On 28 October, Second Panzer Army attempted to storm Tula, but failed to secure it. Between 3 and 13 November, the Soviet 3rd Army attacked Second Panzer Army's right flank at Teploye.

At the end of October, the whole front between Volokolamsk and Maloyaroslavets settled into a relatively quiet period for the next two weeks, as both sides rushed reinforcements and supplies to their forward units. Zhukov had succeeded in delaying a direct German advance upon Moscow, but the Mozhaisk Line was entirely overrun and Army Group Centre had five panzer divisions within 100km of the capital.

The second phase of Operaton *Typhoon* began on 15 November with the Third and Fourth Panzer Armies pushing forward. Third Panzer Army captured Klin on 23 November, while Istra fell to Fourth Panzer Army on the 27th. That same day, Third Panzer Army crossed the Moskva–Volga Canal at Yakhroma. On 1 December, Fourth Army achieved a breakthrough on the Nara River, but the offensive was checked within 48 hours. Heinz Guderian's last attempt to encircle Tula was launched on 2 December, but this too ended in failure.

Operation *Typhoon* was suspended two days later, as extreme winter weather arrived. The speed and ferocity of *Typhoon* had surprised the Soviets once again; but the Soviet defence had not collapsed into a confused rout. Within days, the Soviets would launch the winter counter-offensive by the Kalinin and Western Fronts.

The primary reasons that Operation *Typhoon* failed were serious German operational mistakes, combined with a logistic system that was not up to the task. *Typhoon* was in essence a flawed plan, executed poorly and only initially successful due to the gross ineptitude of the Red Army. Although the Soviets like to claim that they stopped the German offensive, the performance of the Red Army against *Typhoon* was generally weak.

RIGHT The Eastern Front Medal ('Winterschlacht im Osten 1941/42'). This was awarded to German and Axis troops who served on the Eastern Front in the period 15 November 1941 to 15 April 1942, and was instituted on 26 May 1942. Over 3 million were awarded. It was informally known as the 'Frozen Meat Medal' among Axis troops. (Darko Pavlovic © Osprey Publishing)

THE SIEGE OF SEVASTOPOL
30 October 1941–4 July 1942

The Siege of Sevastopol by Axis forces was one of the bloodiest and most brutal battles of the entire war. When it ended in July 1942, only a handful of buildings remained undamaged in the Crimea's largest city, which was home to a strategically vital naval base.

On 13 July 1941, six Soviet DB-3 naval bombers from the Black Sea Fleet's air arm had attacked oil refineries outside Ploesti and set 9,000 tons of oil on fire. Five days later, another attack destroyed 2,000 more tons of oil. The amount of fuel destroyed was enough to provide five loads of fuel for every panzer division in the USSR. The German High Command quickly realized that Sevastopol was a vulnerability that needed to be addressed. Capture of the Crimea, according to Führer Directive No. 33 of 23 July 1941, was now a 'priority mission'.

By mid-November 1941, Sevastopol was the only Soviet foothold left in the Crimea. Gerd von Rundstedt's Army Group South had conquered most of the Crimea in less than a month, a tremendous achievement. However, the German triumph in the Crimea was incomplete as long as fortress Sevastopol was still in Soviet hands. The Soviet High Command was equally resolved to hold on to Sevastopol as a springboard for future offensives and quickly directed reinforcements towards the city.

Sevastopol had a population of 111,000, and thousands of its citizens were drafted to work on three defensive belts around the city before the Germans arrived. The inner defensive line extended out 5–8km from Sevastopol on 4 July 1941, a main defensive line extended out to 10km from the city, and a forward line extended out even farther. Some barbed wire and mines were in place, but the two outer lines were still incomplete when German forces began approaching the city in October 1941.

The Soviet defence was organized into Defensive Sectors, the most important of which were the Belbek River Valley and the western coast (Sector IV), and the hilly area between Kamyschly and Mekenzyya Village (Sector III). Throughout

LEFT German engineers of the 173rd Pioneer Battalion attack Coastal Battery 30, Sevastopol, 18 June 1942. (Howard Gerrard © Osprey Publishing)

the siege the Soviets continued to improve these fortifications, and by May 1942 they presented formidable obstacles.

The commander of the German Eleventh Army, Erich von Manstein, wanted to launch an immediate assault upon Sevastopol before the end of November, but his supply situation was dire. Lacking heavy artillery or effective air support, he decided to avoid the main Soviet defensive positions around the Belbek Valley and to probe for weak spots in the centre of their line. The first German offensive took place between 10 and 21 November, but this failed to achieve a breakthrough, and cost 2,000 men.

On 17 December, von Manstein launched a second offensive headed by Eleventh Army, which lasted five days. The Soviets were forced to pull back to the Belbek Valley. The offensive was abruptly halted by the Red Army's amphibious landings at Kerch in an effort to relieve Sevastopol, gaining a foothold they would retain for the following five months. A long phase of siege warfare now set in around Sevastopol.

Once the Soviet winter counter-offensives had ended in early 1942, Führer Directive No. 41, dated 5 April, ordered 'mopping up operations in the Kerch Peninsula and the capture of Sevastopol'. By now, von Manstein knew that Sevastopol would be a hard nut to crack and he prepared for a deliberate and sustained assault that could gradually rip through its defences. Operation *Störfang* (*Sturgeon Haul*) would be assisted by a massive superiority in artillery and air support. Unlike a typical German campaign based upon manoeuvre, *Störfang* was based upon firepower.

Before dealing with Sevastopol, von Manstein decided to deal with the three Soviet armies located in the Kerch Peninsula, which had been constantly trying to break out. The resulting offensive, *Trappenjagd* (*Bustard Hunt*), began on 8 May 1942, and resulted in a rapid Soviet collapse, smashing the three armies in less than two weeks. In the end, the Soviets only evacuated 37,000 troops from Kerch before it fell, and suffered 28,000 dead and 147,000 captured.

The German *Störfang* operation would be led by the infantry (supported by Italian and Romanian units), organized into assault groups supported by engineers and artillery. Their role was to break through the by now formidable Soviet temporary and permanent defences. Heavy artillery would also be used, including two massive 280mm railway guns. The Luftwaffe contributed VIII Air Corps' bombers and fighters.

Störfang began with a massive aerial assault: the Luftwaffe flew thousands of sorties and had dropped over 25,000 tons of high-explosive and incendiary bombs by the time the ground assault began on 7 June. The infantry slowly ground its way through the Soviet defensive positions, bunkers and large forts, inflicting heavy casualties. Soviet shipping in the port was hammered by Luftwaffe attacks, and many vessels were sunk or capsized. Despite the increasing toll of Luftwaffe attacks, the Black Sea Fleet continued to ship in reinforcements and materiel.

On 23 June, the Soviet defensive line in the north collapsed. Three days later, the Soviet defences on the Sapun Ridge, the final Soviet line between the Germans and the city itself, were overrun. By the morning of 30 June, it was obvious to both sides that Sevastopol's defences had been hopelessly compromised. The final heavy German assault on the city began the following day, spearheaded by LIV Army Corps. By evening on 4 July, organized Soviet resistance had ended, and Eleventh Army finally took the city.

The siege of Sevastopol was costly for both sides. The Soviet Independent Coastal Army was annihilated, and of the

approximately 118,000 Soviet Army and Navy troops who served in the area in June 1942 about 95,000 were captured when the city fell and 5,000 wounded were evacuated; some 18,000 died in the final battle. Losses among Sevastopol's civilian population were severe. Nor had victory been cheap for Eleventh Army. Total German casualties during Operation *Störfang* were at least 4,264 killed, 21,626 wounded and 1,522 missing, for a total of over 27,000 casualties. The Romanian units suffered 8,445 casualties (1,597 killed, 6,571 wounded and 277 missing).

The Germans held Sevastopol for less than two years. In May 1944, the advancing Soviet armies re-entered the Crimea and trapped five German divisions at Sevastopol; some 31,700 German and 25,800 Romanian troops were killed or captured. Soviet troops found that Sevastopol was virtually destroyed after two sieges.

LEFT A lieutenant-colonel from the Romanian 7th Mountain Rifle Battalion, 1942. (Horia Serbanescu © Osprey Publishing)

THE ATTACK ON PEARL HARBOR
7 December 1941

Pearl Harbor remains one of the most iconic events of the war, a day, in the words of US President Franklin D. Roosevelt, 'that will live in infamy'. In the early morning of 7 December 1941, hundreds of Imperial Japanese Navy aircraft pre-emptively struck the island of Oahu in Hawaii, home of the US Pacific Fleet, in an effort to limit American interference in Japan's South-East Asian operations that were being simultaneously launched. The Japanese attack on Pearl Harbor plunged a shocked United States headlong into the war.

US–Japanese relations had deteriorated during the 1930s, and an attack on Pearl Harbor had been planned for some time by Admiral Yamamoto Isoroku, commander of the Japanese Combined Fleet, under the codename Operation Z. The Japanese task force – comprising six aircraft carriers (*Akagi*, *Kaga*, *Soryu*, *Hiryu*, *Shokaku* and *Zuikaku*), two battleships, three cruisers, and 11 destroyers – had departed from the Kurile Islands on 20 November, while diplomatic

LEFT The USS *Nevada* heads for the open sea, pursued by 'Val' dive-bombers, 9.00am, 7 December 1941. (Adam Hook © Osprey Publishing)

negotiations were ongoing between Japan and the United States. Five Imperial Japanese Navy submarines, each embarking a Type A midget submarine, would also travel to Oahu to take part in the operation. Emperor Hirohito finally approved the attack plan on 1 December 1941.

Early in the morning of 7 December, at a point 275 miles north of Hawaii, the fighters ('Zeros'), torpedo planes ('Kates') and dive-bombers ('Vals') that would strike the Pacific Fleet and air stations took off from the decks of the Japanese carriers. They would hit Oahu in two separate waves. The Japanese aircrews targeting US ships were ordered to select high value ones first (aircraft carriers and battleships) followed by any other ships such as destroyers or cruisers.

On the morning of the attack, throughout Oahu limited numbers of personnel were on duty: it was a sleepy Sunday morning – a deliberate part of the Japanese planning.

The first and largest wave of Japanese aircraft, comprising 200 planes, arrived at Pearl Harbor just before 7.50am. Complete surprise was achieved. A US radar technician had picked up the Japanese planes on his radar, but had ignored them because a flight of US bombers was due into Oahu from the United States around the same time. These 12 B-17s arrived while the attack was ongoing, and were attacked by Japanese aircraft as they attempted to land.

Four major battleships lying at anchor in Battleship Row were badly damaged during the opening minutes of the attack; the other four capital ships on the row would also be hit. The USS *Arizona* suffered the greatest devastation: a bomb hit one of her magazines, causing a massive explosion that killed 1,177 of her crew. When the USS *Oklahoma* was struck by torpedoes at 7.56am and capsized, 429 of her crew lost their lives. She would never return to duty, and would be salvaged in 1943. Other US vessels that were damaged included three cruisers and three destroyers.

The second, smaller wave of 170 Japanese aircraft arrived over Oahu one hour 30 minutes after the first wave. The planes were divided into three groups, and arrived over Pearl Harbor from different directions almost simultaneously.

Beyond the ships of the US Pacific Fleet in Pearl Harbor, the air stations at Hickam and Wheeler fields (both belonging to the US Army), and Ford Island (US Navy) were primary targets for the Japanese attack. Secondary targets, to be attacked with any remaining munitions after the primary targets had been dealt with, were Kaneohe Naval Air Station, Bellows Field (US Army), and Ewa Marine Corps Station. All would suffer damage on 7 December, although Bellows Field escaped lightly, being attacked by a solitary aircraft. Most of the US aircraft were closely lined up outside their hangars on 7 December, in compliance with an order to protect them from sabotage. Fuel tanks were low, and many US fighters had also had their machine guns removed, again to avoid sabotage or for routine weekend maintenance.

The three US Pacific Fleet aircraft carriers were not present in Pearl Harbor at the time of the attack. The expectation that the Philippines would be attacked first by the Japanese had resulted in numerous aircraft being transported to Midway and Wake Islands.

Some US fighters did manage to get airborne during the attack. Three P-40s that took off from Bellows Field were quickly shot down by the Japanese. Several P-36s from Wheeler Field were more successful, and did manage to engage the enemy aircraft. Among the US heroes of the day were pilots Kenneth M. Taylor and George Welch, who shot down seven Japanese aircraft between them.

At 10.00am, aircraft of the first Japanese attack wave returned to the task force and began landing on the carriers positioned 260 miles north of Oahu. The Japanese believed that they had done well enough and decided not to launch a third attack wave; the task force turned to withdraw.

Japanese losses were minimal in view of the victory achieved: 64 killed (it is not known how many were wounded). American losses were high: 2,390 killed (2,108 Navy/Marines, 233 Army and 49 civilians) and 1,178 wounded (779 Navy/Marines, 364 Army, and 35 civilians). The largest US ships that were sunk comprised USS *Arizona* (which accounted for half the naval casualties), *California*, *Oklahoma* and *West Virginia*. Many more received bomb and torpedo hits, and would take time to repair, allowing for modernization in the process.

Over 160 US aircraft were lost during the attacks on the various Army, Marine and Naval air stations around Oahu. Japanese aircraft losses amounted to nine 'Zero' fighters, 15 'Val' dive-bombers, and five 'Kate' torpedo planes. Five midget submarines were also lost during the attack. Total Japanese casualties amounted to 55 airmen and nine midget submarine crewmen. One Japanese sailor, Kazuo Sakamaki, was captured after his midget submarine *HA-19* ran aground on Waimanalo Beach, Oahu – the first Japanese prisoner of war to be captured by US forces.

The day after the attack, US President Franklin D. Roosevelt urged the US Congress to formally declare war on Japan. It did so, and three days later both Germany and Italy declared war on the United States, a move that was immediately reciprocated. The United States was now fully committed to war.

BELOW B5N2 'AI-311'of Lieutenant-Commander Shigeharu Murata, the best torpedo-bomber pilot in the IJNAF at the time of the Pearl Harbor raid. (Jim Laurier © Osprey Publishing)

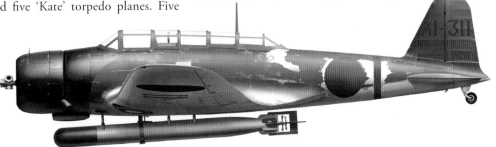

THE MALAYAN CAMPAIGN

8 December 1941–31 January 1942

The Malayan Campaign pitted the British 88,000-strong Malaya Command (comprising Indian Army, Malay, Australian and British troops, under Lieutenant-General Arthur Percival) against the 70,000 invading troops of the Japanese 25th Army (under Lieutenant-General Tomoyuki Yamashita). Its final act, the fall of Singapore, witnessed the largest surrender of British-led forces in history. It was, in the words of Winston Churchill, one of Britain's 'worst military disasters'. Casualties were immense for the British – totalling 138,708 – of which more than 130,000 were prisoners of war.

Singapore and Malaya formed the strategic centre of gravity for the British in the Far East. The presence of a significant naval base and several airbases meant they could dominate South-East Asia.

The fall of France in June 1940 meant that French possessions in Indo-China came under the control of the Vichy Government. The Japanese were soon able to gain approval from the Vichy French authorities to occupy first northern Indo-China, and later, in July 1941, southern Indo-China. This greatly increased the threat to Singapore since it placed Japanese air and naval bases within easy range of the fortress island.

In November 1940, the Japanese received a secret British report which stated that Britain would be unable to send strong reinforcements to Singapore in the event of war. In mid-1941, in order to gain the resources needed to support its war economy (and overcome American, British and Dutch embargos), Japan resolved to seize Malaya and the Dutch East Indies.

Although the British were militarily stretched to the limit in late 1941, they still believed that Singapore could be defended and much had been done to bolster its defences. However, with the British pressed to maintain the security of the sea lanes in the Atlantic, defend the Home Islands from attack, and protect their key position in Egypt, there was little hope of providing significant reinforcement to the Far East.

LEFT Japanese G3M2 Navy Type 96 bombers torpedo HMS *Prince of Wales*, 10 December 1941. (Peter Dennis © Osprey Publishing)

On 4 December 1941, the Japanese invasion convoys bound for the Malayan Peninsula departed from Hainan Island. The British received the first reports of these convoys two days later, with forces in Malaya and Singapore alerted.

A proposed British operation to counter any Imperial Japanese perceived threat to Malaya (Operation *Matador*) was under discussion. *Matador* foresaw a Japanese landing on the east coast of Thailand followed by an advance south to Jitra and Kroh, which British forces could intercept within Thailand, giving time for a main force to assemble and attack the Japanese. However, as late as 6 December Malaya Command believed such a pre-emptive attack to be premature, and it was not actioned.

The Japanese coordinated landings at Singora and Patani in southern Thailand took place on 8 December 1941; the token Thai resistance was quickly overcome. Landings also took place at Kota Bharu in north-east Malaya, and these were more forcefully resisted by Indian Army troops. That same day, Japanese bombers conducted their first raid on Singapore in the south, and launched a series of raids against British airfields in northern Malaya.

Kota Bharu airfield and town were captured by the Japanese on the 9th. Further Japanese invasion forces crossed the border into Malaya from Singora in southern Thailand that evening.

Japan's military action extended into the waters of the South China Sea. On 10 December 1941, off Kuantan, HMS *Prince of Wales* and the battlecruiser HMS *Repulse* became the first capital ships to be sunk solely by air power on the open sea. British sea power in the Far East was greatly weakened as a result.

The fighting in Malaya intensified on 11 December. At Jitra in the north-west the British suffered a major defeat. British fighters under the control of Far East Air Force (RAF) were withdrawn to defend Singapore and its supply convoys, giving the Japanese air superiority over the north of the country. On the north-west coast, the island city of Penang was evacuated by the British on 16 December, and was in Japanese hands by the following day. The decision to withdraw fully from northern Malaya and retreat behind the Perak River was taken on 18 December.

On 29 December, the British made a stand to defend the centre of the country. This was the best opportunity Percival had to derail the Japanese plan for a quick victory. A successful stand here offered the strategic depth to create the conditions for a British counter-offensive. Following a four-day battle at Kampar in west-central Malaya, British forces were forced to retreat to avoid encirclement on 4 January 1942, heading to defensive positions anchored on the Slim River. Here, on

7 January, a Japanese tank attack destroyed two Indian brigades, with the Japanese taking 3,200 prisoners and capturing huge amounts of equipment. The defeat doomed any British attempts to hold central Malaya, and the decision to withdraw to Johore in the south of the country was taken on 8 January.

The defence of northern Johore was another disaster for the British. Two brigades, including the Indian 45th, were destroyed, and the momentum of the Japanese attacks was not blunted.

On the 25th, British commanders took the decision to retreat to Singapore Island. Significant British reinforcements arrived in Singapore in the form of the 18th Infantry Division on 29 January. The last British troops to cross the causeway from Johore into Singapore Island did so on 31 January.

In early February 1942, the Japanese began their bombardment of Singapore, and at 8.00pm on the 8th, the Japanese 5th and 18th Divisions began their attack across the strait, gaining a foothold on the island the following day. On 10 February, Japanese pressure and British command confusion prompted British troops, whose morale was now low, to withdraw from the Jurong Line, the best defensive position outside Singapore.

The inevitable Japanese attack on the city began on 14 February. It was directed along two axes into Singapore, while air raids and artillery barrages pummelled the defenceless city and its population. To compound matters, there was a growing water shortage crisis. With little hope remaining, on 15 February, Percival met with Yamashita and signed the documents of surrender. The Japanese victory presaged the invasion of Burma and later India, and the fall of the Dutch East Indies.

RIGHT A soldier from the 2nd Battalion, Argyll and Sutherland Highlanders, which fought in the Malayan Campaign. (Kevin Lyles © Osprey Publishing)

THE SECOND BATTLE OF KHARKOV

12–28 May 1942

The Second Battle of Kharkov was one of the costliest battles for Soviet forces during the war, with almost 300,000 casualties suffered. A Soviet army group, cut off inside the Barvenkovo pocket, was exterminated from all sides by German firepower.

In early 1942, after the German defeat at Moscow, the Soviet High Command pressured Marshal Semyon Timoshenko, commander of the South-Western Front, to recapture Kharkov, which had fallen to the German Sixth Army on 24 October 1941. At the start of the war, Kharkov was the fourth-largest city in the Soviet Union, with a population of 833,000. It was also the industrial centre of the Ukraine and an important rail transportation hub.

On 1 January 1942, Timoshenko had launched an offensive with four armies to conduct a double envelopment of Kharkov from the north and south. Over several weeks of

brutal fighting, this had managed to tear a great hole in Army Group South's front. For the next two months, Army Group South was forced to fight a desperate battle to contain the Soviet breakthrough. Following reinforcement, Timoshenko's offensive made further progress and created the Barvenkovo salient. However, by mid-February, it was clear that Timoshenko's forces were nearly spent and Army Group South was finally able to establish a very thin defence around the Barvenkovo salient. After a final, unsuccessful Soviet push, less intense fighting continued around the salient throughout March and April 1942, before the spring thaw imposed an operational pause upon both sides. When the weather cleared, both the Red Army and the Wehrmacht intended to launch a major offensive that would decide the issue at Kharkov.

Soviet offensive planning for May 1942 was based on the three armies from South-Western Front conducting a dual pincer attack, from the Barvenkovo salient and from the Staryi Saltov bridgehead, bludgeoning their way through the German defences towards Kharkov. Timoshenko optimistically hoped to complete the encirclement of Kharkov and the German

LEFT German howitzers engage Soviet Matilda tanks in the streets of Nepokrytaya, 12 May 1942. (Howard Gerrard © Osprey Publishing)

Sixth Army within 15 days of the beginning of the offensive. However, Stalin's impatience for action resulted in another hastily planned attack with inadequately trained and supplied forces, and the plan lacked unity of command.

One of the operational prerequisites in the German planning for May 1942 was the destruction of Timoshenko's armies in the Barvenkovo salient. This was known as Operation *Fridericus*, and comprised a classic pincer attack against the base of the Barvenkovo salient, using assault groups from Sixth Army and Army Group von Kleist. However, Army Group South's strained logistical situation made planning for a large-scale offensive difficult. Operation *Fridericus* would also have to share resources with Operation *Trappenjagd* in the Kerch Peninsula in the Crimea. Yet Army Group South's commander Field Marshal Fedor von Bock was in no rush: he would only attack when he had the best prospects for victory.

The Soviet offensive, one of the largest Soviet set-piece offensives of the war to date, was launched on 12 May 1942 with a dual pincer movement from the Volchansk and Barvenkovo salients. The Soviets achieved a successful breakthrough, and had advanced 10km by the end of the first day. The Soviet 28th Army captured Peremoga and encircled Group Grüner in Ternovaya on the 13th, but was shattered two days later by a counter-attack from the German 3rd Panzer Division. The Soviet 21st Army encircled Murom, and heavy fighting also took place around Efremovka.

However, by 14 May the Luftwaffe's IV Air Corps had gained air superiority over the Kharkov sector, and aviation support had been drafted in from the Crimea. The Soviet offensive began to grind to a halt in the face of withering close-air support attacks, while Luftwaffe air supply missions helped hard-pressed German units to hold out.

The German counter-offensive, Operation *Fridericus*, was launched at 5.00am on 17 May. A well-planned artillery preparation was followed by devastating Luftwaffe raids and then III Army Corps' ground attack, which tore a hole in the Soviet 9th Army's front. The 3rd Panzer Division fought its way through to Ternovaya to relieve Group Grüner on the opening day, and the following day von Kleist's Panzers reached the southern part of Izyum. On 19 May, the Soviet 21st Army at Murom was forced to retreat by Kampfgruppe Gollwitzer's advance. As the Soviets were forced back, the Luftwaffe targeted the bridges over the Donets River to hamper retreating Soviet forces.

On 19 May, Timoshenko regrouped his forces into Army Group Kostenko inside the Barvenkovo salient. The following day, he halted Sixth Army's northern offensive, realizing that his forces within the Barvenkovo salient were in dire peril as the German Sixth Army reoriented itself to defeat the pocket. By 22 May, von Kleist's Panzers had linked up with LI Army Corps, cutting off Army Group Kostenko. Over the following days, the 3rd and 23rd Panzer Divisions attacked the northern side of the Soviet Barvenkovo pocket, and were joined on the 24th by German VIII Army Corps and Romanian VI Corps. The remnants of Army Group Kostenko, desperately attempting to fight their way out, were now pulverized by German artillery and air attacks. By 28 May, organized resistance within the pocket ended, prompting Timoshenko to order all other forces in the South-Western and Southern Fronts to shift to the defence. Operation *Fridericus* had been a complete success.

Timoshenko's South-Western Front had suffered a catastrophic defeat at Kharkov. All told, 16 rifle divisions, six cavalry divisions and four tank brigades were annihilated. Another dozen divisions were badly mauled and needed to be pulled out of the line for rebuilding. Of the 765,000 Soviet troops committed to the May 1942 operation, a total of 277,190 became casualties – a 36 per cent loss rate. The Germans claim to have captured 239,000 prisoners. Perhaps the most shocking thing about the Kharkov debacle was the loss of vital command cadre. In contrast to other encircled Soviet armies in 1941–42, the collapse of the Barvenkovo pocket was so rapid that virtually no senior commanders escaped.

Axis personnel losses during the Kharkov Campaign were nearly 30,000, including at least 5,853 dead and 2,912 missing. Friedrich Paulus' Sixth Army suffered 45 per cent of the total casualties.

RIGHT A Soviet T-34/76. The T-34 was the mainstay of Soviet armoured forces throughout the war. (Jim Laurier © Osprey Publishing)

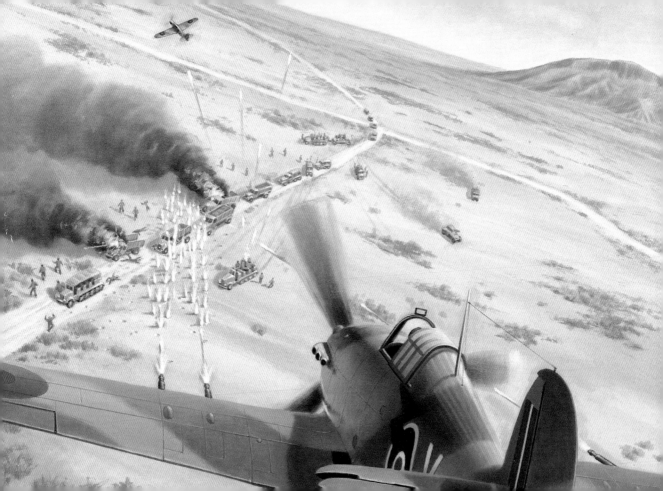

THE BATTLE OF GAZALA
26 May–21 June 1942

The Battle of Gazala is considered the greatest victory of General Erwin Rommel's career. Rommel and his fledgling Afrika Korps had been dispatched to North Africa in early 1941, in an effort to support beleaguered Italian forces and restore some prestige to the Axis cause. The Western Desert became a full-scale theatre of war, in which British and Commonwealth forces and Axis troops gained and lost vast extents of terrain in a series of fluctuating battles and fortunes.

By the start of January 1942, most of Rommel's forces were ensconced in their former positions (from where they had advanced ten months previously) along the El Agheila–Marada strongpoint facing eastwards. They were ready to fight a defensive battle against Lieutenant-General Neil Ritchie's advancing Eighth Army, whose morale had been boosted by the successes of Operation *Crusader*. However, on 21 January Rommel launched a surprise attack, and in just over two weeks, and with almost negligible losses, the Axis commander had

driven Eighth Army back over 560km and had retaken much of the ground lost during *Crusader*. By 4 February, the retreat had become a flight and Eighth Army was compelled to withdraw into prepared positions at Gazala, 64km to the east of Tobruk.

Between February and May 1942, a lull ensued, during which both sides rested, trained their forces and prepared to launch new offensives. Rommel and General Sir Claude Auchinleck (Commander-in-Chief Middle East) both knew that the other would attack when ready.

On 26 May, Rommel seized the initiative and opened his Gazala offensive. His attack was focused on the northern section of Eighth Army's line and was led by the Italian Group Crüwell. Early on the following day, Rommel led a mobile armoured force around the southern flank of the British line, attempting to drive into its rear. Lieutenant-General Ritchie countered this move using his armoured brigades, and managed to slow Rommel's forward movement.

On 29 May, Rommel decided to concentrate his armour in an area known as 'the Cauldron'. This position was virtually

LEFT A British Hurricane attacks an Afrika Korps convoy at Gazala. (John White © Osprey Publishing)

surrounded by the British Eighth Army, but Rommel understood that he could strike eastwards from this area when the time was right. As he withdrew into this position, his rear came into contact with a defended 'box' manned by Brigadier Haydon's 150th Brigade, which was soon eliminated. Rommel also daringly opened up supply routes to the west through the British minefields.

Ritchie believed that he had Rommel's forces trapped in the Cauldron, and launched new attacks from 30 May to crush the Afrika Korps. However, they lacked sufficient concentration of force and were easily repulsed by the Germans. Moreover, the opening up of a direct supply route eastwards through the minefields meant that Rommel's forces were no longer surrounded.

On 3 June, while holding the British armour in the centre, Rommel dispatched forces southwards to attack the Free French outpost at Bir Hacheim. This was overrun and captured a week later.

In the meantime, on 5 June Ritchie launched Operation *Aberdeen* to crush Rommel's position in the Cauldron. Rommel's troops held off the attack, and then launched a counter-attack against the British armoured formations, which succeeded in driving off three armoured brigades and capturing large numbers of infantry.

On 11 June, Rommel once again concentrated his mobile forces and moved against the centre of the British rear. His attack was met by the British XXX Corps, led by Lieutenant-General Charles Norrie, and halted, but with great losses to the British tank force.

The following day proved to be the decisive one in the Gazala fighting. A great clash of armour took place on the 12th to the south of 'Knightsbridge' (one of the British rear defensive positions). The losses that the British incurred forced a withdrawal to the north and east, leaving those formations of Eighth Army to the west vulnerable. On 13 June, the 201st Guards Brigade was forced to retreat from the Knightsbridge position in the centre of the British line, and Rommel's forces began to pick off the isolated British and Commonwealth positions west of Tobruk. The 50th and 1st South African Divisions began to withdraw from the Gazala Line on the 14th, and Eighth Army was now in danger of collapse.

Rommel's forces reached the coast to the east of Tobruk on 17 June, and once again the strategically vital port was surrounded. All units of Eighth Army that were able to do so now began a retreat back to the Egyptian border. Tobruk was attacked from the east by the Afrika Korps on 20 June, and a break-in was soon achieved. The Axis forces quickly spread out within the fortress area, and on 21 June the garrison surrendered.

German troops pursued the retreating Eighth Army back across the frontier into Egypt as June ended. Auchinleck understood the gravity of the situation, with Egypt in great danger of being overwhelmed, and on 25 June he relieved Ritchie as the head of Eighth Army and placed himself in control. Eighth Army withdrew first into the defences south of Mersa Matruh, where Auchinleck fought a delaying action. By 30 June, all remaining Eighth Army units had retired further eastwards behind the El Alamein defensive line – very much the last-ditch position. Although disorganized, exhausted and confused, Eighth Army was still intact and with a framework of command on which it could be rebuilt to its former strength.

Rommel's Afrika Korps was also exhausted, but renewal and replenishment were unlikely for his tired formations, for they had stretched their lines of supply and communication virtually to breaking point. They had outrun their air cover, used nearly all of their fuel and ammunition and had run their tanks into the ground. Although Rommel was pressing the British, his troops were in no fit state to launch what could be the decisive battle of the campaign. The two tired armies now looked at each other across the desert at El Alamein and prepared for what was to be the final showdown.

RIGHT Shown here in 1943, this major wears the typical arrangement of the desert uniform for officers of the Afrika Korps. (Raffaele Ruggeri © Osprey Publishing)

THE BATTLE OF MIDWAY
4–7 June 1942

Midway was unquestionably the most dramatic and important battle of the Pacific War. At Midway Atoll, 1,300 miles northwest of Oahu in Hawaii, the Imperial Japanese Navy was dealt a major defeat in its attempt to eliminate the US Pacific Fleet and capture the strategically important island. Midway marked the end of the Japanese expansion phase, and although the Japanese Navy was far from a beaten force, the battle clearly defined the next stages in this theatre.

In April 1942, the Japanese found themselves facing a key strategic decision. Until now, they had enjoyed an unparalleled string of successes in their campaigning. Assuming the defensive was unthinkable, and so two courses of action were open to them: seizing the key islands in the South Pacific to cut the sea lines of communications between the United States and Australia; or advancing in the Central Pacific with the ultimate goal of seizing Hawaii. What resulted from the

strategic debate between the Navy General Staff and the Combined Fleet was a fatal compromise. In May, limited operations would be conducted in the South Pacific with the goal of seizing the strategic airfield at Port Moresby on New Guinea, to be followed in June by a massive operation against the US-held atoll of Midway and against selected points in the Aleutian Islands chain.

Unfortunately for the Japanese, the commander of the US Pacific Fleet, Admiral Chester Nimitz, was determined to engage the Japanese aggressively as soon as favourable conditions existed, as demonstrated in the Battle of the Coral Sea, fought between 7 and 8 May 1942. The clash was the first ever contest fought between and decided by aircraft carriers, and exacted a high cost from both sides: the Japanese saw all three carriers engaged at Coral Sea removed from the order of battle for the forthcoming Midway engagement, while the US Navy was left with only two fully operational carriers in the Pacific.

The operation to invade Midway and engage the remaining strength of the US Pacific Fleet would be the

LEFT Dive-bombers from USS *Enterprise* and *Yorktown* attack the Japanese carrier *Hiryu* at Midway, 4 June 1942. (Howard Gerrard © Osprey Publishing)

ultimate effort of the Japanese Navy. All eight of its operational carriers were committed, as well as the fleet's 11 battleships. Of 18 heavy cruisers, 14 were assigned roles in the operation, as were the bulk of the navy's light cruisers and destroyers. This force was under the command of 28 admirals. The navy's largest operation of the war would consume more fuel than an entire year of normal operations.

On 27 May 1942, the 1st Mobile Force (a combined carrier battle group) departed the Inland Sea to begin the Midway operation. Most significantly, the element of surprise had been lost: the Americans had intercepted and decoded Japanese messages and were able to determine the date and location of the forthcoming attack. As a result, on 28 May the carriers USS *Enterprise* and *Hornet* departed Pearl Harbor, to be followed two days later by USS *Yorktown*. The US carriers rendezvoused north-east of Midway on 2 June.

The first sightings of the Japanese battle group came on 3 June at 8.43am, when Midway-based PBY Catalina planes spotted the Japanese Minesweeper and Transport groups. These were attacked by US aircraft over the course of that day and into the next.

On 4 June, at 4.30am, Vice Admiral Nagumo Chuichi ordered the launch of a 108-aircraft strike against Midway; two hours later the first bombs struck the atoll, inflicting heavy damage for the loss of 25 Japanese aircraft. The Americans were quick to react, and at 7.00am 116 aircraft took off from the carriers *Enterprise* and *Hornet* to attack the Japanese carrier group, alongside fighters and bombers from Midway.

The Japanese lead officer of the first strike against Midway informed Nagumo around this time that a second strike would be needed against the atoll, and at 7.15am Nagumo ordered his reserve aircraft into action. Meanwhile, US aircraft continued to attack the Japanese carriers, without inflicting damage. By 8.30am, the Japanese had become aware of the presence of US carriers in the area. Nagumo altered his plans just after 9.00am to instead target the American carriers.

At 10.22am, a large group of dive-bombers from USS *Enterprise* attacked the carrier *Kaga*. Four hits were scored, causing mortal damage. Minutes later, VB-3 from *Yorktown* (comprising 17 Dauntless dive-bombers) struck the *Soryu*, with three hits causing uncontrollable fires. Then, at 10.26am, three Dauntlesses attacked *Akagi*, and with a single hit caused her damage that ultimately proved fatal.

At 12.09pm, dive-bombers from *Hiryu* began their attack on the *Yorktown*, scoring three hits. *Yorktown* was set afire and temporarily came to a stop. At 2.43pm, torpedo aircraft achieved two hits on *Yorktown*, bringing the ship to a halt once more and causing a severe list.

At 5.05pm, *Hiryu* was attacked by US dive-bombers from *Enterprise* and *Yorktown*; four hits set the Japanese ship afire. Two hours later, just after 7.10pm, the *Soryu* sank, followed minutes later by the *Kaga*. The *Akagi* sank the following morning at 5.20am, as did the *Hiryu* at 8.20am. The *Yorktown* followed them to the bottom on 7 June at 5.01am. The other major losses during the battle were the *Mikuma*, a Japanese heavy cruiser sunk while heading for Wake Island on 6 June, and USS *Hammann*, which went down while assisting the sinking *Yorktown*.

There was no disguising the fact that the Japanese had been dealt a major defeat. All four of the 1st Mobile Force's carriers had been sunk and all aircraft on those ships (248 in total) had been lost. The total number of Japanese dead stood at 3,057 personnel. The landing on Midway was never attempted.

The Americans suffered a total of 144 aircraft lost and 362 sailors, Marines and airmen killed. In a single encounter, the US Pacific Fleet had blunted the offensive strength of the Imperial Japanese Navy and altered the balance of power in the Pacific. Before Midway, the Japanese had the advantage of a numerically superior carrier force; after Midway, this was no longer the case.

RIGHT Lieutenant-Commander E.E. Lindsey and his rear-seat gunner Aviation Chief Radioman C. T. Grenat flew this Douglas TBD-1 'Devastator' from USS *Enterprise* in the morning strike against the Japanese carriers off Midway Atoll on 4 June 1942. (Tom Tullis © Osprey Publishing)

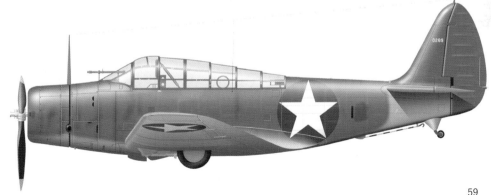

THE BATTLE OF GUADALCANAL

July 1942–February 1943

Guadalcanal was the first major Allied offensive against the Japanese in the Pacific War. When American Marines stormed ashore at several points in the southern Solomon Islands on 7 August 1942, it was the start of an epic struggle between Japan and the US, which would last over six months.

After their successful operation at Pearl Harbor in December 1941, the Japanese had little trouble conducting what they called the First Operational Phase: the occupation of the Philippines, Malaya, the Dutch East Indies, Burma and Rabaul on the island of New Britain in the South Pacific. The next step, and the goal of their Second Operational Phase, was to create strategic depth for their new possessions. Most of the expansion was planned for the South Pacific, including eastern New Guinea, Fiji, Samoa and 'strategic points in the Australian area'. The Japanese had to decide how to sequence their operations, and there were sharp differences of opinion about how to proceed between the Army and Navy, and within the Navy itself. The compromise reached planned for operations beginning in the South Pacific in early May 1942, against Midway and the Aleutians in early June, and then an invasion to seize Port Moresby on New Guinea and occupy Tulagi Island in the southern Solomons.

Despite defeat at the Battle of the Coral Sea on 7–8 May 1942, the first phase of the Japanese Solomons operation went according to plan, resulting in the occupation of the island of Tulagi on 3 May. Tulagi was useful as a seaplane base and gave the Japanese their first foothold in the area. Tulagi was not big enough for an airfield, but it was located some 32km north of a virtually unknown island named Guadalcanal.

On 6 July 1942, a 12-ship Japanese convoy arrived off Lunga Point on northern Guadalcanal with two construction units to start work on an airfield. With long-range aircraft based on Guadalcanal, the Japanese could threaten Allied supply lines to Australia and New Zealand.

Following Midway, Admiral Ernest King, Commander-in-Chief US Fleet, planned to shift to the offensive. On

LEFT The first Japanese attempt to retake Henderson Airfield on Guadalcanal, 21 August 1942. (Peter Dennis © Osprey Publishing)

24 June, he directed Admiral Nimitz to come up with a plan to capture Tulagi and nearby islands. Guadalcanal and its nascent airfield was added as an objective on 5 July. The operation was given the codename *Watchtower* and would be led by the 1st Marine Division under Major-General Alexander Vandegrift.

On 22 July, the 1st Marine Division departed Wellington in New Zealand. The first landings took place on Guadalcanal on 7 August and encountered no resistance. The following day the incomplete airfield on the island was captured.

The Americans suffered a significant setback on the night of 8/9 August, when the Imperial Japanese Navy inflicted a savage defeat on the US Navy in the waters off Guadalcanal in the Battle of Savo Island. The Japanese sank four heavy cruisers (three American and one Australian) and damaged another without loss. The transports were forced to depart Guadalcanal before the unloading of vital supplies had finished.

The first Japanese destroyer arrived on Guadalcanal on 16 August carrying 113 Japanese marine reinforcements. Two days later, a three-company sortie across the Matanikau River by the US 5th Marines, known as the First Battle of the Matanikau, resulted in severe losses for the Japanese. The Matanikau River would be the site of several major clashes during the long battle for Guadalcanal, with the Americans attempting to clear stubborn pockets of Japanese troop concentrations.

The key to the Marines' survival was completing the airfield. Using mostly captured Japanese equipment and tools, it was finished on 18 August and named Henderson Field. The first echelon of Marine Air Group 23 landed on the newly completed airfield on 20 August. Several unsuccessful Japanese attempts to seize Henderson Field would take place, beginning 20–21 August.

The fighting continued into September 1942. On the 12th, the Battle of the Bloody Ridge (also known as Edson's Ridge) began, with the Japanese launching attacks against the US Marines' positions there.

Throughout October, the Japanese continued to bring in reinforcements, in preparation for a major ground offensive: some 15,000 troops landed on the island between 1 and 17 October. The Americans were also bringing in reinforcements: on 13 October the men of the 164th Infantry Regiment became the first US Army troops to enter the campaign.

The planned Japanese offensive was launched on 24 October, attacking from south of Henderson Field near the east bank of the Lunga River. Over two nights, the

Japanese attempted several frontal assaults on the US positions, but suffered over 1,500 casualties for little gain. The attacks were cancelled, and the Japanese retreated back to the Matanikau Valley.

Between 13 and 15 November, the naval battles of Guadalcanal took place. Despite suffering heavy losses, the Americans managed to ward off Japanese attempts to bombard Henderson Field using battleship gunfire.

By December, the Japanese supply situation was becoming desperate, with many garrison troops on the point of starvation. Combat deaths, injuries and tropical diseases were all taking

their toll. On 26 December, the decision was taken to evacuate all Japanese army and navy forces from Guadalcanal. However, the first evacuation run would not take place until 1 February 1943. Just under 11,000 Japanese troops would eventually make it off the island.

Between January and February 1943, the Americans conducted several offensives to clear the island of Japanese troops. They gradually advanced across Guadalcanal, and by 9 February, all organized Japanese resistance had ended.

The six-month campaign for Guadalcanal proved to be one of the most pivotal in the Pacific War. For the Americans, it showed that the Japanese Army could be defeated, even in the jungle, but it also showed what difficult opponents the Japanese could be. The Japanese Army had shown itself to be incapable of defeating a modern opponent: an army built around fighting spirit could not defeat one built on firepower.

Of the 31,400 Japanese troops that reached the island, around 20,000 became casualties, mostly from disease. The Americans suffered 1,207 Marines and 562 Army soldiers killed during the long battle.

LEFT A rifleman of the 5th Marines, Guadalcanal, 1942. (Peter Dennis © Osprey Publishing)

THE BATTLE OF STALINGRAD
23 August 1942–2 February 1943

Stalingrad remains the largest and bloodiest battle in the history of warfare, and it was one of the key turning points of World War II. On the banks of the Volga River, the Red Army fought and defeated (at enormous cost) one of the largest and best-equipped army formations on the Eastern Front at that time – Friedrich Paulus' Sixth Army.

According to the planning for *Case Blue* (*Fall Blau*) – the Wehrmacht's 1942 strategic summer offensive in southern Russia – German forces would advance with a two-pronged attack: Operation *Edelweiss* comprised a move on the Axis right flank over the Caucasus Mountains to seize the Baku oilfields, while Operation *Fischreiher* would see an advance on the left flank along the Volga River towards the city of Stalingrad. On 9 July 1942, Army Group South was split into Army Groups A and B, with A tasked with *Edelweiss*, and B (under Field Marshal Maximilian von Weichs, and containing

German, Hungarian, Italian and later Romanian armies) with *Fischreiher*. Hitler's Directive No. 45 on 23 July 1942 stated that Stalingrad and the Caucasus were to have equal priority and were to be attacked simultaneously.

The Soviets had deployed their retreating 62nd and 64th Armies (part of the recently formed Stalingrad Front) in a bend in the Don River to the west of Kalach, with the aim of impeding Sixth Army's advance on Stalingrad. Army Group B crashed into these units at the Battle of Kalach, between 25 July and 11 August. Despite some initial defensive setbacks, the Germans managed to drive into the Soviet flanks, successfully collapsing the Soviet positions and forcing their withdrawal across the Don River towards Stalingrad.

By 10 August 1942, German forces had cleared most Soviet resistance to the west of the Don, but this, plus supply problems, delayed Army Group B's advance on Stalingrad itself. By this point, the Soviet High Command had realized that the Stalingrad Front was too large to control from a single headquarters, and so a new South-Eastern Front, under Colonel-General Andrey Yeryomenko, was formed to take

LEFT German troops from the 79th Infantry Division assault the Red October Steel Plant at Stalingrad, 23 October 1942. (Peter Dennis © Osprey Publishing)

command of its southern sectors. Yeryomenko was given responsibility for the defence of Stalingrad itself.

On 19 August, Paulus ordered Sixth Army to advance on Stalingrad, and his army crossed the Don on 23 August. Meanwhile, Fourth Panzer Army headed up from the south through Kotelnikovo. Paulus' advance was cautious, with his army's movement restricted by fuel shortages. Repeated Soviet counter-attacks on Army Group B's northern flanks also slowed progress. Within a few days, Sixth Army had reached the outskirts of the city, linking up with Fourth Panzer Army on 2 September.

On 14 September, the first German assault on Stalingrad began, as Sixth Army tried to force its way into the centre, with Fourth Panzer Army securing the southern flank. From this point, Sixth Army was drawn into an attritional battle, with vicious street fighting inside the long, stretched-out, riverside city. Stalingrad was subjected to intense artillery and air bombardment, which would result in its almost complete destruction. The Soviet defensive strategy was to stay close to the advancing German forces, so that their air and artillery support advantages were negated.

On 27 September, the second German assault on the city began, grinding its way slowly forward. The Soviets had brought in so many reinforcements to the Stalingrad and South-Eastern Fronts that by 28 September a further reorganization was required, and the Don Front was created, under Lieutenant-General Konstantin Rokossovsky.

On 14 October, the third German assault on the city was launched. Slowly, the Soviet defenders were forced into four shallow bridgeheads on the Volga's western bank. By 19 November, Sixth Army was in control of almost all of the decimated city.

It was at this point that the Soviets launched Operation *Uranus*, the offensive to encircle and destroy the Sixth and Fourth Panzer Armies in Stalingrad, commencing 19 November. Overwhelming numbers of Soviet troops attacked the weakened and thinly held German flanks, manned by exhausted Romanian, Hungarian and Italian troops, which soon collapsed. Four days later, on 23 November, Soviet forces from the South-Eastern and Stalingrad Fronts met at the town of Kalach, completing the encirclement of 290,000 troops of the German Sixth Army and Fourth Panzer Army within Stalingrad. A smaller-scale Soviet operation to complete the isolation of Sixth Army from Army Group Don, *Little Saturn*, was launched on 16 December.

The German IV Air Fleet tried desperately to ferry supplies into the beleaguered Sixth Army, but there were simply not enough transport aircraft available to move the kind of tonnages

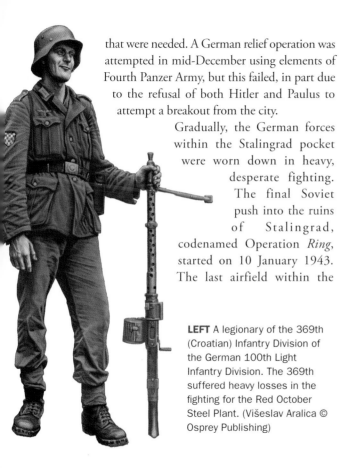

that were needed. A German relief operation was attempted in mid-December using elements of Fourth Panzer Army, but this failed, in part due to the refusal of both Hitler and Paulus to attempt a breakout from the city.

Gradually, the German forces within the Stalingrad pocket were worn down in heavy, desperate fighting. The final Soviet push into the ruins of Stalingrad, codenamed Operation *Ring*, started on 10 January 1943. The last airfield within the German pocket fell on 16 January, and with it the last hope for Sixth Army vanished. On 26 January, forward elements of the Soviet 21st and 65th Armies made contact with the 13th Guards Division near Mamayev Kurgan, and split Sixth Army in two. A northern German pocket formed around the factories, while to the south a larger pocket formed between Mamayev Kurgan and the Tsaritsa River.

Running out of ammunition and food, on 31 January 1943, Paulus surrendered with the forces in the southern pocket. On 2 February, the remaining German forces in the northern pocket followed suit. The five-month battle for Stalingrad was over.

German casualties in the battle for the city itself were just under 300,000 troops (of whom 150,000 were killed), with another 300,000 casualties suffered by the remaining German forces of Army Groups A, B and Don. Italy suffered over 110,000 casualties, the Romanians 160,000, and Hungarians 143,000. The Soviets lost over 1.2 million troops, of whom 478,700 were killed. Hundreds of thousands of civilians also lost their lives.

Stalingrad was virtually destroyed during the fighting. The city was awarded 'Hero' status in 1945, and in 1961, under Nikita Khrushchev's programme of destalinization, it was renamed once again as Volgograd.

LEFT A legionary of the 369th (Croatian) Infantry Division of the German 100th Light Infantry Division. The 369th suffered heavy losses in the fighting for the Red October Steel Plant. (Višeslav Aralica © Osprey Publishing)

THE EL ALAMEIN BATTLES

1 July–11 November 1942

The battles which took place in the desert to the south of the isolated railway station of El Alamein in 1942 marked the climax of Hitler's plan to wrest Egypt from the British. His goal of seizing the Suez Canal and opening the Middle East to Axis forces had to be abandoned when his forces were soundly beaten. The Allied successes precipitated the collapse of Field Marshal Erwin Rommel's Panzer Army, forcing it into a long retreat across North Africa.

After its hurried retreat eastward following Rommel's victory in the Battle of Gazala, the exhausted British Eighth Army took up positions on the El Alamein line on 30 June 1942. The equally weary advance units of Rommel's Panzer Army Africa brushed up against it the same day. Both sides now squared up to each other across kilometres of barren desert and quickly prepared for a decisive showdown. However, it would take three separate battles before a result could be declared.

LEFT The 3rd King's Own Hussars advance during Operation *Supercharge*, 2 November 1942. (Howard Gerrard © Osprey Publishing)

The first of the El Alamein battles was fought between 1 and 27 July 1942, and comprised two weeks of disparate actions fought by two exhausted armies, each trying to regain the upper hand. On 1 July, Rommel launched an infantry attack against the Alamein 'box' defended by the 90th Light Division and sent his Afrika Korps round its flank. However, both attacks failed to dislodge the British. On 9 July, he attacked again, in the south of the line, using the tanks of the 21st Panzer and Italian Littorio Divisions, but once again this failed to create a breakthrough. Allied counter-attacks began, and on 14 July the Australian 9th Division captured Tel el Eisa near the coast, while the following day the New Zealand Division launched an unsuccessful attack on the Ruweisat Ridge, failing to dislodge Rommel's forces. A coordinated combined Australian, New Zealand and South African attack on Rommel's centre was launched on 21–22 July, and initially was successful, until further countermoves by Rommel's forces eventually drove them back. A final Allied attack took place on 26–27 July, with the Australians pushing south-west from Tel el Eisa towards the Miteirya Ridge. By this time both sides were tired and well-established in defence. The Australian attack failed to shift the enemy and General Sir Claude Auchinleck called a halt. Both he and Rommel realized that further gains were impossible before their forces had rested and replenished their supplies. Both now strengthened their defences and gathered for the next attack. This first battle of El Alamein had stopped Rommel's advance towards Cairo and saved Egypt.

Several changes now took place in the Allied command: Auchinleck was replaced by General Sir Harold Alexander as Commander-in-Chief Middle East, and on 12 August a new commander arrived to take over the British Eighth Army: Lieutenant-General Bernard Montgomery.

The second battle took place at Alam Halfa and comprised Rommel's last, unsuccessful attempt to break through the Alamein line and into Egypt. His attack was launched on 31 August, but after two days of fighting, Axis forces were unable to get past Montgomery's strong defences around Alam Halfa Ridge. Rommel pulled back his army, but his retreat was then hit in the flank by the New Zealand Division, whose counter-attack was beaten off with only minimal losses. Alam Halfa marked the beginning of the turnaround in British fortunes: Rommel was stopped and

the initiative passed to Montgomery. Both sides then spent September and most of October preparing for the battle that became known as El Alamein.

On 23 October, Montgomery fired the largest artillery barrage yet seen in the war and launched Operation *Lightfoot*. The British XXX Corps attacked the northern minefields of Rommel's positions and attempted to carve out an area ready for X Corps to force two corridors through the Axis defences. Once through the German line, Montgomery intended to bring the German armour to battle on his terms. Secondary attacks were also launched in the south by XIII Corps to confuse the enemy. Montgomery's corps in both sectors of the line failed to penetrate the main German defences over the opening days: in the north, the armour of British X Corps was reluctant to advance too far forward of the infantry, despite constant urgings by Montgomery to galvanize his forces for a supreme effort. On 26 October, the Australian 9th Division began to carve out a salient around Point 29 in the north, while 1st Armoured Division attacked Kidney Ridge to the south of the Australian effort.

The following day, 27 October, Rommel launched a counter-attack against 1st Armoured Division with his Afrika Korps, but was checked by the British division's anti-tank guns. Similar attacks against the Australians were also

turned back. From 28 October, Montgomery switched his main effort to the north and used the Australian Division to carve out a salient towards the coast. Rommel countered this move by shifting more of his armour northwards.

Montgomery's final battle to break through Rommel's positions at Alamein, Operation *Supercharge*, began late on 1 November with an attack by the reinforced New Zealand Division. At 6.15 am the next day, behind a rolling barrage, 9th Armoured Brigade took up the advance with orders to break through the enemy anti-tank and field-gun positions to 'hold the door

LEFT The NCO commander of an American 'Lend Lease' M4 Sherman from 7th Armoured Division, El Alamein, October 1942. (Mike Chappell © Osprey Publishing)

open' for the 1st Armoured Division of X Corps. The advance by the 3rd King's Own Hussars is recognized as one of the greatest armoured regimental actions of the entire war. The Hussars faced fierce enemy opposition and shellfire and by its end were left with just seven serviceable tanks out of the 35 that had set off that morning. But the regiment had gained its objective and broken through the Axis anti-tank line along the Rahman Track, allowing X Corps a route through the German defences. It was the turning point of Operation *Supercharge*, and more and more of Eighth Army's divisions began to fight their way through.

By 4 November, it was clear that Montgomery had won at El Alamein, and Axis forces started their retreat, streaming back towards the coast road and heading for the Egyptian border. By 23 November, Rommel found himself back where he started in January 1942 at El Agheila.

El Alamein was Montgomery's greatest triumph, and Rommel was finally defeated in a stand-up fight. Prime Minister Winston Churchill later claimed that before Alamein the British Army had not gained a major victory; after Alamein it did not suffer a major defeat. However, Rommel's forces had been allowed to slip away along the coast of North Africa, avoiding a potential Eighth Army *coup de grace*.

THE BATTLE FOR TUNISIA

17 November 1942–9 May 1943

The Battle for Tunisia was a vital operational proving ground for the Allies in preparation for the forthcoming liberation of Europe. It also witnessed the destruction of Rommel's Afrika Korps, and the loss of precious troops and materiel for the Axis: the term 'Tunisgrad' (mirroring Stalingrad) was coined for the defeat.

The Anglo-American plan for new North African operations in late 1942 sought to squeeze the Axis forces out of North Africa from the west, while the British and Commonwealth forces pursued them westwards through Libya following the victory at El Alamein. The Allied landings in French North Africa (Operation *Torch)* would be conducted at three locations by a primarily American force. When the landings took place in November 1942, the reaction of the Vichy French forces present was mixed. Although there was some resistance in a few locations, by and large the landings took place without serious opposition. Following the German and Italian occupation of Vichy France, the French Army of Africa joined the Allies.

By mid-November 1942, Axis forces in Tunisia began to grow in number. Hitler dispatched a German contingent under General Nehring to occupy a Tunisian bridgehead. A race developed to see who would seize Tunisia first: Lieutenant-General Kenneth Anderson's First US Army, marching from Algeria, or the Fifth Panzer Army, arriving in Tunisia by aircraft and ship from Italy. The Germans won the race, and by mid-December, a stalemate had developed along the Tunisian frontier, with the Allies still too weak to overcome the Wehrmacht defences, and the German forces too poorly supplied to drive the Allies back into Algeria.

Disregarding instructions that he stage a last-ditch defence of Libya, Rommel managed to extricate most of the German units and some of the better Italian units into Tunisia by February 1943, shielded behind the French-built Mareth Line. Despite his being ordered back to Germany to recuperate from exhaustion and health problems, and his

LEFT The charge of the 1st Armored Regiment at Sidi Bou Zid, 15 February 1943. Only four US tanks survived. (Michael Welply © Osprey Publishing)

command being turned over to the Italian General Giovanni Messe, Rommel understood that the Allied defences in Tunisia were still weak, and the southern flank was held by inexperienced American forces: he believed that a hard blow would easily puncture the American lines.

The Allied plan for the Tunisian Campaign called for Allied forces to move between the key deep water port cities of Bizerte and Tunis, capture the latter as soon as possible, then surround Bizerte and build up sufficient force to bring about its surrender.

On 30 January 1943, the Fifth Panzer Army pushed back French and US forces from the Faïd Pass, the principal route from the eastern branch of the mountains into the coastal plains. The Allied forces withdrew to a new defensive line at the town of Sbeïtla.

On 11 February, the Italian High Command issued instructions for an offensive in Tunisia by Rommel's Panzer Army Africa and General Hans-Jürgen von Arnim's Fifth Panzer Army. Instead of a unified attack directed by Rommel, two complementary attacks would be conducted separately by von Arnim and Rommel. Von Arnim would lead Operation *Frühlingswind* (*Spring Wind*) and surge out of Faïd towards Sidi bou Zid, destroying Combat Command A (CCA) of the 1st Armored Division. Rommel would launch the second spoiling attack, dubbed Operation *Morgenluft* (*Morning Breeze*) that would take Gafsa, 100km to the south, thereby ending any threat to the rear of the Mareth defences.

Frühlingswind was launched three days later with an attack on CCA of the US 1st Armored Division at Sidi bou Zid. An attempted US counter-attack at Sidi bou Zid was crushed on the 15th, and the CCA withdrew to Sbeïtla until forced out of there on 17 February. On 16 February, Operation *Morgenluft* began: it encountered little opposition, and Gafsa was taken as planned. Reconnaissance elements of Rommel's battlegroup and von Arnim's forces met at Kasserine on 18 February.

At midnight on 18 February, the Italian High Command authorized Operation *Sturmflut* (*Stormflood*) led by Rommel, who had both the 10th and 21st Panzer Divisions shifted to his command. The plan was for Rommel to strike north-west through the Kasserine Pass towards the key road junction at Thala and Le Kef, ultimately heading for the Allied supply centre in the city of Tébessa. Von Arnim was ordered to support Rommel's attack by tying down Anderson's forces in northern Tunisia, and by staging a paratroop drop near Le Kef to destroy key bridges and prevent Allied forces from retreating.

Rommel's command began its assault against the US and French defences in the Kasserine Pass early on 19 February.

It was unable to break through on the first day of the attack, and at nightfall fighting continued on both sides of the pass, with the Germans trying to infiltrate past the defences through the mountainous terrain. By the evening of the following day, the Germans had finally opened a way through the pass.

The Allies sent the US 1st Armored Division's CCB to block the route to Tébessa for the advancing Germans on 21 February. Also that day, the 10th Panzer Division fought a bloody, day-long battle against stiff British defences on the approach to Thala. By 22 February, the German attack along the Tébessa Road had gone awry, and the attack on Thala had been halted by artillery fire. With news arriving that the British Eighth Army were about to reach the Mareth Line, the German retreat eastward to support the Mareth defences was ordered at 2.15pm that afternoon.

On 25 February, Allied forces reoccupied the Kasserine Pass, followed on 17 March by Gafsa. Gradually, the Allies forced the retreating Germans back into a pocket along the northern-central Tunisian

coast. On 7 May, the British 7th Armoured Division captured Tunis, and the following day the key port of Bizerte fell to Allied forces. On 9 May, the US 1st Armored Division reached the Mediterranean, and the Fifth Panzer Army surrendered, followed on 13 May by the remaining German forces in Tunisia. Over 275,000 Axis troops had been captured. The defeat of the Italian Army in Tunisia, combined with the enormous losses suffered in the Stalingrad campaign, marked the end of any serious role of the Italian armed forces in Axis war planning.

RIGHT An M3 Medium Tank of Company D, 2/13th Armored Regiment, Tunisia, December 1942. (Hugh Johnson © Osprey Publishing)

THE BATTLE OF KURSK

12 July–23 August 1943

At Kursk in 1943, the Wehrmacht launched its final strategic offensive on the Eastern Front. For the first time, a major German offensive was halted before it could break through the Soviet defences and reach its strategic depth. The battle began with the German Operation *Zitadelle* (*Citadel*) on 5 July, which sought to remove the Kursk salient in a pincer move, and ended with the Soviet counter-attack Operation *Kutusov* against the rear of the German forces in the north.

After the German Sixth Army had been encircled and destroyed at Stalingrad, the Red Army launched a series of powerful counter-offensives that pushed Army Group South back all along the line and forced the Germans to abort their campaign in the Caucasus. By February 1943, Soviet armour had liberated Kharkov and was approaching Dnepropetrovsk. For a moment, the German position in southern Ukraine was on the verge of complete collapse. However, Field Marshal

LEFT Operation *Kutusov*, 12 July 1943. The torrent of T-34s and infantry smashed through the Germans' main line of resistance near Ulyanovo in the north. (Steve Noon © Osprey Publishing)

Erich von Manstein was able to mount a desperate counter-attack that recaptured Kharkov on 14 March 1943 and brought the Soviet advance to an ignominious halt. Nevertheless, the Soviets were left in possession of the Kursk salient, which protruded into the boundary between Army Groups Centre and South.

By late March it was evident that the Red Army would enjoy a large numerical superiority in armour for the upcoming summer campaigns. It was questionable whether the Wehrmacht could regain the strategic initiative under these conditions. Nevertheless, after partially rebuilding Army Group South, Hitler intended to conduct a limited objective offensive in the summer of 1943, and the elimination of the Soviet-held Kursk salient by means of a classic combined-arms pincer attack (led by von Manstein's Fourth Panzer Army in the south, and General Walter Model's Ninth Army in the north) seemed feasible. The two pincers would meet at Kursk.

Facing Model in the north were the armies of General Konstantin Rokossovsky's Central Front. To the south, opposing von Manstein, were the armies of the Voronezh Front, under General Nikolai F. Vatutin. Soviet defensive capabilities had improved greatly by early 1943: the Red Army had the time (thanks to British intelligence intercepts) to create larger, denser minefields that were covered by direct fire, as part of much deeper defensive belts. The Soviets also knew where the attacks would be coming from, and had time to bring in large numbers of reserves.

Model's northern operations for *Zitadelle* began early on 5 July with the German Ninth Army's advance into three Soviet defensive belts, supported by artillery and the Luftwaffe. The dense fortifications slowed the German advance, but a 10km penetration was achieved on the first day. Rokossovsky committed part of Central Front's 2nd Tank Army to a counter-attack on 6 July, which developed into extended fighting around the villages of Ponyri and Olkhovatka between 7 and 10 July. By 9 July, it had become clear to Model that Ninth Army lacked sufficient strength to make a breakthrough, and the following day, with the attack grinding to a halt, Model suspended its *Zitadelle* offensive.

The southern pincer moves of Operation *Zitadelle* by von Manstein's Fourth Panzer Army also began on 5 July, pushing into the heavy Soviet defensive belts, heading for the village of Gertsovka. The following day, XLVIII Panzer Corps reached the Soviet second line of defence on the Pena River. II SS-Panzer Corps also made good progress, breaking through the first line of defence and advancing 20km. The Voronezh Front quickly committed all its reserves, but was struggling to contain Fourth Panzer Army's advance.

On 7 July, XLVIII Panzer Corps attacked the Soviet 3rd Mechanized Corps near Dubrova. The concerned Soviet High Command ordered the 5th Guards Army and 5th Guards Tank Army (part of its strategic reserve) to begin moving towards the Voronezh Front at this point. On 8 July, Vatutin launched a counter-attack with four tank corps against II SS-Panzer Corps, but this failed to gain ground. On 10 July, the axis of the German advance shifted towards Prokhorovka. Vatutin ordered the 5th Guards Tank Army and 1st Tank Army to counter-attack II SS-Panzer Corps at Prokhorovka early on 12 July, which resulted in a massive armoured clash.

On 13 July, Hitler ordered Operation *Zitadelle* suspended: the Allies had just invaded Sicily, and forces would need to be transferred to Italy. However, von Manstein was allowed to continue limited attacks for several more days.

Sensing a slowing of the German operational tempo, the Soviets launched Operation *Kutusov* on 12 July, with over 1.2 million troops and 2,400 tanks. *Kutusov* was directed against the Orel salient in the north, held by Army Group Centre, and

was led by the Soviet Western (attacking from the north) and Bryansk (attacking from the east) Fronts. A key aim was to encircle and destroy the German Ninth Army. Significant penetrations were achieved in some sectors in the opening days, and the size of the salient was reduced. The Soviet High Command committed further forces to *Kutusov* between 15 and 26 July, including the Central Front and the Soviet 3rd and 4th Guards Tank Armies.

On 31 July, in order to avoid being encircled, Hitler authorized Model's battered

LEFT This female sniper from the Red Army is armed with a Moisin Model 1891/30 rifle. (Ron Volstad © Osprey Publishing)

Ninth Army to evacuate the Orel salient. The resultant Operation *Herbstreise* (*Autumn Journey*) began the following day. *Kutusov* continued into August, with the city of Orel liberated on 5 August, and the reduction of the Orel salient. Operation *Kutusov* was brought to an end on 18 August. Altogether, the Soviet Central, Western and Bryansk Fronts suffered a total of 429,890 casualties during *Kutusov*, but it achieved far more than the failed German *Zitadelle* operation.

Although Kursk is often called the 'greatest clash of armour in history', much of the fighting was dominated by mines, infantry combat, artillery and air attacks. German planning for *Zitadelle* was seriously flawed at both the operational and tactical levels, failing to anticipate the effect of water obstacles and often dissipating combat power across diverging axes of attack. Soviet defensive tactics were much improved at Kursk, with Soviet mine warfare proving a great success that deprived the Panzers of much of their mobility.

In the south, the Soviets launched a companion offensive on 3 August, codenamed Operation *Polkovodets Rumyantsev*, seeking to retake Belgorod and Kharkov and inflict heavy damage on Army Group South. The operation was a Soviet success, with both cities being recaptured. Army Group South would soon be pushed back towards the Dnepr River.

THE BATTLE OF MONTE CASSINO

17 January–18 May 1944

The Battle of Monte Cassino comprised a series of Allied assaults against the German Gustav Line defences on the Italian Peninsula. The operations to secure the area around the ancient abbey cost the Allies over 55,000 casualties, with the Germans suffering some 20,000 killed and wounded.

Following the Axis surrender in North Africa, the Allies landed in Sicily on 10 July 1943, securing the island two months later. On 3 September, Montgomery's British Eighth Army crossed the Straits of Messina and landed on the toe of Italy. Mussolini's government had already fallen and on 8 September a new Italian administration announced Italy's surrender. The next day, the US Fifth Army landed at Salerno, and the British V Corps came ashore at Taranto.

New German divisions were immediately moved across the Italian border and the country was swiftly brought under the heel of the Third Reich. Field Marshal Albert Kesselring

was responsible for defending the whole country as Commander Army Group C.

The Allied forces in southern Italy (under General Sir Harold Alexander) comprised British, American and Canadian troops, as well as a French expeditionary corps, New Zealand and Indian Army divisions, and a Polish corps. During the autumn of 1943, Lieutenant-General Mark Clark's US Fifth Army advanced northwards from its Salerno beachhead along the western coastal strip, while the British Eighth Army drove up the east coast alongside the Adriatic Sea.

Kesselring decided to use the Sangro and Garigliano rivers as the anchor of a strong defensive line across Italy: the Gustav Line. It took three months for both Allied armies to fight their way up to this line, arriving there in December 1943, where they paused and regrouped ready for a spring attack.

The Allied plan was for the French Expeditionary Corps to attack in the mountains to the north of Cassino in the region of the upper Rapido River, towards Belmonte Castello and Atina, and then swing southwards into the Liri Valley well beyond Monte Cassino. Focus would then switch to the south where the British X Corps would attack with three divisions across the Garigliano River and into the Aurunci Mountains. Then the US II Corps would put in the most important assault, attacking across the Rapido River in the Liri Valley to form a bridgehead. A combined battlegroup would then pass through the bridgehead and strike out towards Rome, linking up with the Allied landings at Anzio en route.

On 12 January 1944, the French Expeditionary Corps moved into the mountains north of Cassino and made contact with the defences of the Gustav Line. After four days of fighting, General Alphonse Juin's corps was forced to a halt. The US Fifth Army's assault on the Gustav Line began on 17 January, with the British X Corps attacking across the Garigliano River and the French trying once more to break into the German fortifications. After days of fighting, in which some gains were made, both attacks ground to a halt in the face of severe enemy resistance.

On 20 January, the US 36th Infantry Division attacked across the Rapido River in an attempt to break into the Liri Valley, but was forced back after heavy losses in two days of fighting. Attempts to cross the Rapido continued on 24 January, as the US II Corps attempted to push its 34th Infantry Division across north of the town of Cassino, behind the defences around Monte Cassino, and into the Liri Valley. The attack was initially successful and American troops managed to move onto the high ground to the rear of Cassino; however, they were halted on the hills close to Monastery Hill.

On 15 February, General Bernard C. Freyberg and his New Zealand II Corps were given the task of capturing Cassino and Monte Cassino. The battle began with the complete destruction of the monastery by heavy bombers. The two divisions then attacked: the Maori Battalion managed to capture Cassino's railway station, but was then forced out by a German counter-attack, while the 7th Indian Brigade failed to even capture its start line.

On 15 March, Freyberg attacked again, beginning with the complete destruction of the town by Allied bombers. Freyberg then attacked down the Rapido into the town, but even after eight days of fighting his forces were still unable to evict the German 1st Parachute Division from the ruins. On the flanks of Monte Cassino, the 4th Indian Division occupied Castle Hill and the Gurkhas seized Hangman's Hill just under the walls of the monastery, before the division was forced to retreat nine days later.

Between mid-March and early May, the Allies made preparations for a major offensive against the Gustav Line.

Alexander brought over the bulk of the British Eighth Army from the Adriatic Front. His new attack, codenamed Operation *Diadem*, would see four corps advance simultaneously. The main thrust would be by the British XIII Corps up the Liri Valley, where it would join up with the US VI Corps, the latter having broken out of the Anzio lodgement.

Operation *Diadem* began on 11 May 1944. The US II Corps attacked from its Garigliano bridgehead and advanced up Route 7, while the French Expeditionary Corps pushed through the Aurunci Mountains and then swung down into the Liri Valley. The following day, the British XIII Corps crossed the Rapido River, broke through the Gustav Line and swept up towards a new German defensive line called the Hitler Line.

The ruined monastery on top of Monte Cassino dominated the battlefield around Cassino. It looked down on both the approaches to the town and into the Liri Valley, while the other side of the valley was anchored by the enemy-held Aurunci Mountains, which overlooked Route 6 – the road to Rome. On 12 May, the Polish II Corps began a series of attacks to seize Monastery Hill. The Germans had held onto the barren knoll at the southern end of Snakeshead Ridge since January 1944. The carefully defended position on a bare outcrop of rock could only be taken by hand-to-hand fighting, and the lines were so close together that artillery fire and mortars could not be effectively used. Each German had to be winkled out of his stone redoubt by physical force. Eventually, on 17 May, after days of intense fighting, the Poles managed to occupy the monastery ruins.

French, Canadian and British troops attacked the Hitler Line on 23 May, and two days later the line started to crack. The Germans began their withdrawal towards Rome.

RIGHT A warrant officer from the 26th Battalion, 2nd New Zealand Division, which fought at Cassino in 1944. (Mike Chappell © Osprey Publishing)

THE BATTLE OF IMPHAL
8 March–3 July 1944

The fighting that took place around Imphal in 1944 involved over 200,000 British, Commonwealth and Japanese troops. It marked a turning point in the Burma Campaign, and was the largest defeat on land for the Japanese to that date.

The town of Imphal was the capital of the princely state of Manipur in the extreme east of India, and stood on its border with Burma. The Imphal Valley (or Plain), at an altitude of some 800m, was the only large stretch of flat ground in the mountainous terrain that defined the India–Burma frontier, and provided a vital passage between the two countries. It acquired considerable importance once the Burma Road (used to send supplies to General Chiang Kai Shek's forces battling the Japanese in China) was cut in 1942.

In early January 1944, the Imperial General Headquarters in Tokyo authorized a pre-emptive attack on India, a cause that had for some time been championed by Lieutenant-

General Mutaguchi Renya, commander of the Japanese 15th Army. The primary objective of the resultant Operation *U Go* was the capture of Imphal.

The Japanese 15th Army's total strength at the start of the operation was around 84,000. Two of its infantry divisions would be engaged at Imphal, the 15th (15,000 men) and the 33rd Division (18,000 men). A third division – the 31st (15,000 men) – would advance on Kohima to the north. The remaining 36,000 men were army troops, while another 4,000 or so troops arrived as reinforcements as the Imphal battle wore on.

The British Fourteenth Army, under Lieutenant-General William J. Slim, had its IV Corps at Imphal. This consisted of three infantry divisions – the 17th Indian, 20th Indian and 23rd Indian. The 50th Indian Parachute Brigade also arrived in March 1944. As the battle unfolded, reinforcements were flown in from the 5th and 7th Indian Divisions in the Arakan. The total strength of Fourteenth Army at Imphal during the battle was around 120,000. The British XXXIII Corps would also join the fighting in July 1944.

LEFT The fight for 'Gibraltar', so-called after its Mediterranean namesake, on the Shenam Saddle, 24 May 1944. (Peter Dennis © Osprey Publishing)

Imphal can be a confusing battle to follow. In comparison with the simultaneous battle at Kohima, it unfolded over a larger area, and was a vastly more spread-out affair, taking in areas on both sides of the India–Burma frontier. Slim has described the fighting at Imphal as being as bitter as at Kohima, but more diffuse.

In terms of its chronology, the Imphal battle can be broadly understood to have taken place in four stages. The first, from March to mid-April 1944, involved the Japanese laying siege to Imphal and the valley it sits in. The second, from mid-April to May 1944, had the two sides engaged in a battle of attrition. The tide shifted in favour of Fourteenth Army in the third phase in June 1944, while disaster then befell the Japanese in July as they were routed on all the fronts.

Perhaps the best way to grasp the geography of the Imphal battle is to follow an analogy used by Slim himself: he likened Imphal to the hub of a wheel, with the main roads heading out of the town as its spokes. These routes were used by the Japanese in their advance on Imphal. The bulk of the fighting in 1944 took place simultaneously on or around these routes. Indeed, the town of Imphal itself emerged essentially unscathed from the battle, unlike Kohima, which was devastated.

The three broad directions from which the Japanese approached Imphal were, firstly, from the south-west, which included the Tiddim Road and the Silchar Track, from where the 33rd Division came. Secondly, there was the Tamu–Palel Road in the south-east, from where Yamamoto Force (again from the 33rd Division) advanced. Finally, there was the vast region to the north and north-east of Imphal, used by the 15th Division. This included – from east to west – the Ukhrul Road, the Iril River Valley, the Mapao–Molvom Range and the Imphal–Kohima Road.

The Japanese attack at Imphal began well, with the 33rd Division moving forward on 8 March 1944. Mutaguchi managed to cut off (albeit without destroying) the 17th Indian Division on the Tiddim Road and drew reserves away from Imphal, leaving Lieutenant-General Geoffrey Scoones' IV Corps suddenly vulnerable. The Japanese thrust from the north via the 15th Division was a surprise for the British, but they quickly brought in reinforcements in the form of two brigades of the 5th Indian Division from the Arakan. These units began plugging the gaps in the northern defences. On 26 March the Japanese took Nippon Hill on the Shenam Saddle (the Tamu–Palel Road) for the first time: the saddle would be the scene of intense fighting and change hands several times. The Imphal–Kohima Road was cut on 29 March, and Imphal entered a state of siege.

A battle of attrition ensued between April and May 1944. Scoones had managed to concentrate the divisions under his command in and around the Imphal Valley by 4 April. About a fortnight later, the Japanese had been held on all of the spokes leading to the hub at Imphal. In the period that followed, both sides faced each other in the hills and the valley in a gruelling test of will and stamina.

On the night of 20/21 May, the Japanese attempted to seize the position known as Gibraltar, the most precipitous of the hills on the Shenan Saddle. Although their initial attacks were beaten off, the one on the night of 23 May succeeded and the Japanese gained possession of Gibraltar's crest. The fate of the entire Shenam Saddle now hung in the balance, but the very next day the hill was recovered following a counter-attack led by the 5/6th Rajputana Rifles and 3/10th Gurkha Rifles. Gibraltar was the farthest the Japanese would be able to advance on the Shenam Saddle and the closest they came to breaking through.

By June, at all points of the compass around Manipur, the military advantage had slipped in favour of Fourteenth Army, and the Indian, Gurkha and British battalions were slowly beginning to make gains. On 22 June, the 5th Indian Division and British 2nd Infantry Division met on the Imphal–Kohima Road and ended the siege of Imphal.

On 16 July, the last Japanese stronghold in the Imphal Valley was taken, and Mutaguchi ordered a phased withdrawal of his exhausted soldiers. Thousands of Japanese troops died in the retreat of 15th Army in July towards the relative safety of the Chindwin River. The failure to capture Imphal shattered Mutaguchi's army, and the clock began to tick on the Japanese hold on Burma.

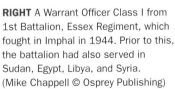

RIGHT A Warrant Officer Class I from 1st Battalion, Essex Regiment, which fought in Imphal in 1944. Prior to this, the battalion had also served in Sudan, Egypt, Libya, and Syria. (Mike Chappell © Osprey Publishing)

THE NORMANDY LANDINGS

6 June 1944

Codenamed Operation *Neptune* and often referred to as D-Day, the Normandy landings witnessed the largest seaborne invasion force ever to be assembled. *Neptune* was part of the larger Operation *Overlord*, the Allied invasion of Occupied Europe.

One of the initial dilemmas was the target for Operation *Neptune*. The Pas de Calais opposite Dover was the narrowest point of the English Channel and the most obvious target. Normandy was the next most likely area, as the Bay of the Seine offered some shelter from weather, there were sufficient beaches with characteristics suitable for amphibious assault, and it was less likely to be heavily defended. German commanders believed that the Allies would launch several smaller amphibious attacks to draw off German reserves from the main landing. This greatly confused German defence plans and restricted the actions of German theatre commanders.

LEFT US assault troops during the second wave of landings at Easy Red Beach at Omaha, 6 June 1944. (Howard Gerrard © Osprey Publishing)

The 80km section of the Normandy coast that was targeted for the landings was divided into five sectors: Utah, Omaha, Gold, Juno and Sword. British and American airborne operations would also be used to seize key objectives on the eastern and western flanks in support of the beach assaults.

The landings on Gold Beach were the responsibility of British forces. They began at 7.25am on 6 June, and once ashore, the British infantry cleared several fortified urban areas adjacent to the beach in house-to-house fighting. Two major gun emplacements were also disabled at Gold, using specialized tanks. By the end of 6 June, 24,900 troops had been landed at Gold, together with 2,100 vehicles and thousands of tons of supplies, for the loss of around 1,000 casualties.

The Canadian Army was tasked with Juno Beach. Initial heavy resistance was encountered from the German 716th Infantry Division defenders in the first minutes of the landings, but within two hours most of the coastal defences had been cleared. The Canadians then began their push inland towards Carpiquet and the Caen–Bayeux railway line, reaching further inland than the other D-Day landing forces.

At Sword, the easternmost beach, the British-led landings encountered light opposition. However, the 3rd Infantry Division's exit from the beach was delayed due to congestion, and stronger resistance materialized in the deeper German defensive positions. The 21st Panzer Division also conducted an armoured counter-attack on D-Day, which further delayed the British breakout. In support, the British 6th Airborne Division captured the Caen Canal and River Orne bridges early on 6 June, and destroyed five other bridges over the Dives River and (temporarily) captured the Merville Gun Battery that threatened the landings on Sword Beach.

The plans for the US Army landings at Utah Beach were a bold attempt to use airborne units to overcome the difficult terrain behind the beachhead. In the largest combat airdrop of the war so far, two airborne divisions were delivered at night behind enemy lines with the aim of securing the key bridges and access points. Due to the inherent risks of such a night operation, the paratroopers were scattered and unable to carry out many of their specific missions. Yet in spite of these problems, the gamble paid off. The landings at Utah Beach encountered light opposition and few German strongpoints, and within a day the US Army had a firm foothold in Normandy.

Of all the landings on D-Day, Omaha Beach was the only one ever in doubt. The beach was much more heavily defended than any of the others and its high bluffs posed a much more substantial defensive obstacle than the relatively flat beaches elsewhere. A classified wartime British study noted that the three beaches in the British/Canadian sector were defended by an average of nine anti-tank guns per beach compared with 30 anti-tank and field guns at Omaha, four mortars per beach compared with six at Omaha and 21 machine guns compared with 85 at Omaha. The preparatory bombardment of Omaha Beach was also shorter than those at the neighbouring British/Canadian beaches, in some cases by as much as an hour, as the Omaha landing took place earlier due to tidal variations.

Access from Omaha Beach was limited to five gullies, called 'draws' by the US Army, and only two of these were readily passable by armoured vehicles or motor transport. These became the centre point of German defences.

The naval shelling of Omaha began at 5.45am on 6 June, lasting for 40 minutes. The first wave of tanks started to land at just before 6.30am, followed minutes later by the first wave of assault troops. Within moments of landing, a third of the assault troops in the first wave had become casualties. With the tide turning, many of the anti-craft defensive obstacles gradually became submerged.

The second wave of troops landed at Omaha between 7.00am and 7.30am. The first advance over the 150ft-high bluffs took place at 7.20am, and over the following hour more US troops followed.

While the second wave was landing at Omaha, US Army Rangers arrived at Pointe-du-Hoc – a 30m-high cliff overlooking Omaha and Utah landing beaches, which the Germans had heavily fortified and which contained an artillery battery. Having climbed to the summit by 7.25am, and despite being isolated from other Allied forces, they held off several German counter-attacks. The Rangers would remain hemmed in overnight, and would not be relieved until the morning of 8 June. By then, only 90 fighting men were left out of their original contingent of 225.

The 14 German strongpoints in the area of Omaha were gradually reduced. At 10.00am, the 18th and 115th Infantry Regiments began landing, adding fresh momentum, and by 11.30am the first exit from the beach had been cleared. By the end of D-Day, the US Army had a firm toehold on Omaha Beach, clinging to a ragged line about a mile inland from the beach. This fell far short of the plan but was, in view of the serious underestimation of German strength, a significant accomplishment. A total of about 34,200 troops landed at Omaha Beach on D-Day.

Over the next seven weeks, the Allies would fight a bitter battle for the *bocage* and the city of Caen, before finally breaking out of Normandy during Operation *Cobra* in the last week of July.

RIGHT The M1926 life belt, issued to US troops for amphibious operations. The lifebelt was automatically inflated by triggering two small carbon-dioxide bottles attached via the screw cap ends. Many of those who landed on D-Day were unable to swim. (Peter Dennis © Osprey Publishing)

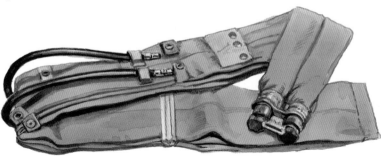

THE BATTLE OF SAIPAN

15 June–9 July 1944

The American plan to capture the three key Marianas islands of Saipan, Tinian and Guam was one of the most ambitious in the history of amphibious warfare. It was to be carried out at vast distances from permanent bases: over 5,500km from Pearl Harbor and 1,600km from Eniwetok.

By the summer of 1944 the Allied counter-offensive in the Pacific was in full swing. The Solomon and Bismarck Islands in the South Pacific had long been secured, as had eastern New Guinea, by General Douglas MacArthur's Southwest Pacific forces. In the Central Pacific, the Gilbert Islands had been cleared the previous year and the Marshalls had been seized. Some bypassed Japanese garrisons remained in these areas, but they were slowly being bombed and starved into submission and posed no threat. The great Japanese naval and air bases at Rabaul on New Britain and Truk in the Marshalls had been neutralized, giving the US Third and Fifth Fleets free rein in

the Central Pacific. In September 1943, the Imperial General Headquarters established Japan's outer defence line running from the Dutch East Indies, through eastern New Guinea, the Carolines, Marshalls and Marianas. However, the thrust into the Marshalls had already penetrated this line. Beginning in April–May 1944, the Allies conducted several landings on the north coast of New Guinea. In the Central Pacific, the Marianas would be the next Allied objective.

The Marianas (comprising 15 islands running north to south in a shallow curving chain) had key strategic value. The US Air Force's new long-range bomber, the B-29, was now being deployed, but the only operating bases within range of Japan were in China. The logistics of transporting ordnance, fuel, spare parts and all the other necessary supplies into China from India were a major difficulty. Airbases in the Marianas would place Japan within a bomber's round-trip range and could be easily supplied by ships direct from the United States.

Out of all the potential airbase sites, Saipan (the second largest island in the Marianas) and Tinian were 160km closer to Japan than Guam. Saipan also had three airfields, all under

LEFT The largest tank battle in the Pacific: Saipan, 16 June 1944. Around 1,000 infantry and 37 tanks were involved. (Howard Gerrard © Osprey Publishing)

construction: Aslito in the south, Charan Kanoa in the south-west, and one in the north at Marpi Point.

On all three Marianas islands, significant Japanese forces were present, under the command of the Northern Marianas Army Group. Japanese troops on Saipan alone amounted to over 30,000 men, almost double US intelligence estimates.

A preparatory naval and air bombardment of Saipan, Tinian and Guam took place on 11–13 June. The invasion of Saipan was given priority and was launched on 15 June 1944, with the US 2nd and 4th Marine Divisions landing on the west of the island, followed by the US Army's 27th Infantry Division, commencing 16 June.

Both Charan Kanoa and Aslito airfields were captured by 18 June and made usable for US fighters, and the American invasion force reached Saipan's east coast. On 20 June, US artillery units began to shell the island of Tinian from Saipan. At the same time, the Battle of the Philippine Sea (known to the Japanese as the Battle for the Marianas) was taking place some 300km west of Saipan, which resulted in an emphatic US naval victory.

Having cleared Japanese forces from the south of the island, the US 2nd and 4th Marine Divisions and the 27th Infantry began to push north through Saipan. The 27th Infantry encountered heavy resistance from the Japanese defenders, and its commander was replaced several times. By 25 June, Mount Tapotchau in central Saipan and the Kagman Peninsula on its central-eastern coast had been seized. The Marines reached the village of Garapan on the western coastline on 30 June, and took the Japanese Seaplane Base at Tanapag on 4 July. The Japanese were now pushed back into the narrowing north of the island.

Among the final battles to take place on Saipan was the 7 July 1944 Japanese *banzai* attack on the 27th Infantry Division. Japanese forces were now holed up in a small valley near Makunsha Village on Saipan's north-west coast, dubbed Paradise Valley by the Americans and Valley of Hell by the Japanese. Before dawn on 7 July, their commander, Lieutenant-General Yoshitsugu Saito, ordered a final *banzai* charge, aiming to fight through Garapan and Charan Kanoa, and then across the island to Nafutan Point, where it was thought that other Japanese troops were still holding out. At 4.00am, an estimated 3,000 Japanese troops charged and overran the American lines, pushing the shocked survivors back to Tanapag. As the Japanese attack began to slow, Saito committed suicide that morning, and the lost ground was regained by early evening. Over 4,300 Japanese dead were found in the area, and over 500 US infantry and Marines were killed. Little Japanese organized resistance remained after the attack.

On 9 July, the 2nd Marines secured Mount Marpi at the same time as the 24th Marines took the airstrip and reached Marpi Point in the far north. Saipan was finally declared secure at 4.15pm on 9 July. However, mopping up operations would continue for several days on the island. A major sweep of Saipan was made with all three regiments of its new US garrison in line, starting north of Tanapag Harbor and moving north, concluding on 5 August.

A final horror experienced on Saipan was the mass suicide of hundreds of Japanese civilians – men, women and children. Many threw themselves and their children off the island's northern cliffs. The Americans attempted to stop them using loudspeakers and Japanese-American linguists, but often to no avail.

The battle for Saipan was a decisive engagement, both militarily and politically. Japan's National Defence Zone was pierced, the Imperial Japanese Navy suffered a critical defeat from which it could not recover, and an American base was secured from which

B-29 bombers could attack the Japanese Home Islands. Although one of the mandated islands, Saipan was considered practically Japanese territory because of its heavy colonization.

The loss of Saipan had both military and political ramifications for the Japanese. On 26 June, well before Saipan fell, Emperor Hirohito requested that his Foreign Minister find a diplomatic way to end the war. The Japanese Government delayed announcing the island's fall, and when it did, Prime Minster, War Minister and Chief of Army General Staff Tojo Hideki and his cabinet were forced to resign on 18 July. The Navy Minister and the Chief of the Navy General Staff also stepped down.

RIGHT A Japanese rising sun flag and 'belt of a thousand stitches', inscribed with best wishes from the soldier's friends and family. (Michael Welply © Osprey Publishing)

THE BATTLE OF THE PHILIPPINE SEA

19–20 June 1944

The encounter in the Philippine Sea was almost exclusively a carrier battle, the fifth of the Pacific War and by far the largest ever fought. Fifteen fleet and light carriers took part on the American side and nine on the Japanese. For sheer size alone, the Battle of the Philippine Sea was the second largest naval engagement of the Pacific War, surpassed only by the Battle of Leyte Gulf fought a few months later.

In line with the planning for the seizure of the Marianas, the US Navy expected a major reaction from the Imperial Japanese Navy. As a result, the destruction of the Japanese carrier fleet was one of the operation's primary objectives. The Japanese Navy had been hoarding its carriers for almost 20 months, and its commitment to defend the Marianas was planned to be a decisive encounter with the US Navy.

Admiral Raymond A. Spruance, commander of the US Fifth Fleet, had the primary mission of conducting the Marianas invasion (Operation *Forager*) and defeating any Japanese naval reaction. Spruance issued his plan on 12 May 1944: the Fifth Fleet's mission was to capture Saipan, Tinian and Guam while being ready to 'drive off or destroy enemy forces attempting to interfere with the movement to or the landing operations at each objective.' To achieve this, Task Force 58 would take up position to the west of the Marianas, ready to respond to any Japanese counter-attack.

On 15 June 1944, in response to the preliminary air and naval attacks on Saipan, Tinian and Guam, the Japanese activated Operation *A-Go* to defend the Marianas. The Japanese First Mobile Fleet, under Vice Admiral Ozawa Jisaburo, departed the Guimaras and entered the Philippine Sea later that day, where it was spotted by an American submarine. Two days later, the fleet was again spotted, this time by the submarine *Cavalla*, 700 nautical miles west of Guam, and by 18 June it was within 400 nautical miles of US Task Force 58. By now, Spruance had decided to await the Japanese fleet and fight a defensive battle.

LEFT US Hellcats from VF-15 flying off USS *Essex* attack a formation of 'Jills' and 'Zeros', 19 June 1944. (Jim Laurier © Osprey Publishing)

A first wave of Japanese search aircraft was launched at 4.45am on 19 June, and gained contact with Task Force 58. The first Japanese strike raid against Task Force 58 comprising 69 aircraft was launched at 8.30am; US radar picked up the raid while still 125 nautical miles distant, and just after 10.20am, Task Force 58 launched all available fighters. The first Japanese attack aircraft were intercepted just over ten minutes later. Only 17 aircraft would eventually return to the Japanese carriers.

The second Japanese strike force, featuring the best-trained aviators in the First Mobile Fleet and consisting of 128 aircraft (48 'Zero' fighters, 53 'Judy' dive-bombers and 27 'Jills' with torpedoes), left the Japanese carriers at 8.56am, and comprised the largest Japanese attack of the day. The flight was detected by US radar at 11.07am. It suffered even greater losses than the first attack wave: a mere 31 planes made it back out of the original 128.

The third attack launched at 10.00am, comprising 15 fighters, 25 'Zeros' with bombs, and seven 'Jills' with torpedoes. From this wave, 40 out of 47 aircraft returned to the ships, chiefly because the contact location given to the aircrews turned out to be erroneous with no US ships present; seven of the returning aircraft were intercepted by US fighters, however, and shot down.

A fourth Japanese attack was launched at 11.00am, comprising 30 'Zero' fighters, ten 'Zeros' with bombs, 36 dive-bombers (27 'Vals' and nine 'Judys') and six 'Jills'. These 82 aircraft were directed at another non-existent contact and, after finding nothing, split into three smaller groups. The final tally was dismal: only nine returned to their carriers, with 30 of them having been shot down over Guam. Despite these heavy losses, no American ships were hit.

Some of the Japanese attack aircraft did make it through to the US ships. In Task Group 58.7, one hit was scored on the battleship USS *South Dakota* and near misses were recorded on two of its cruisers just before 10.50am, from Japanese aircraft in the first attack wave. Around 12.00pm, remnants of the second Japanese attack inflicted minor damage on the carriers USS *Wasp* and *Bunker Hill*.

US submarines also inflicted damage on the First Mobile Fleet. At 9.09am, the Japanese carrier *Taiho* was hit by a torpedo from the submarine *Albacore*, and at 12.22pm the submarine *Cavalla* torpedoed the carrier *Shokaku*. The latter sank just after 3.00pm with heavy loss of life. A massive explosion ripped apart the *Taiho* at 3.32pm, and she followed *Shokaku* to the bottom.

By the end of 19 June, Task Force 58 was heading west to engage the Japanese First Mobile Fleet. Morning searches the following day failed to locate the carrier force, but at 3.40pm it was finally spotted and Spruance decided to launch an all-out attack with 216 US aircraft. Once detected, the First Mobile Fleet took evasive action to the north-west in an attempt to avoid the attack. Between 6.40 and 7.10pm, the US aircraft made a series of hasty attacks on the First Mobile Fleet, striking the carrier *Hiyo* with a torpedo, and damaging two other carriers, two escorts and two oilers. The *Hiyo* sank just after 8.30pm. Shortly after, Vice Admiral Ozawa was ordered to break off action and head for Okinawa, and the following day, Spruance ordered Task Force 58 to abandon its pursuit of the First Mobile Fleet.

The Battle of the Philippine Sea was certainly a decisive encounter. In only ten days in mid-June, the Americans realized all their major objectives and

the Japanese Navy suffered a major defeat. Most of its carriers escaped, but their aircraft and trained aircrews did not. This effectively meant the end of the Japanese Navy as a major threat to future American moves in the Pacific, and led directly to the desperate and ill-conceived Japanese plan to defend Leyte in October that resulted in the final destruction of the Japanese Navy.

The Battle of the Philippine Sea clearly demonstrated to key leaders in the Imperial Japanese Navy that there was no future in conventional air attacks against the US Navy. The solution was the adoption of suicide missions that would increase in ferocity until the end of the war.

RIGHT This F6F-3 Hellcat served with VF-1 aboard USS *Yorktown* during the Pacific War. (Jim Laurier © Osprey Publishing)

THE WARSAW UPRISING

1 August–2 October 1944

From the moment Poland was captured in 1939, the Germans used mass murder to terrorize the Polish population. The Nazi plan first intended to exploit Poland for forced labour and economic resources, and then envisioned the reduction of the ethnic Polish population down to 3 to 4 million within a decade and total extermination within a few decades. In the Soviet-held east, all people in the occupied area were now declared Soviet citizens, and over 1.4 million people from eastern Poland were deported to serve as forced labour in the Soviet Union.

Yet even before Poland was overrun, the Polish Army's General Staff had begun planning to form an underground resistance movement. In early 1940, the Polish Government-in-exile ordered Stefan Rowecki, former commander of the Warsaw Mechanized Brigade, to form a new resistance group, which evolved into the Home Army in February 1942. However, there was never a single Polish resistance movement during World War II, mainly owing to political disunity. Initially, Polish resistance activities were focused on conducting sabotage against German rail traffic, propaganda activities to undermine German morale, clandestine weapons production and intelligence collection.

The brutal German occupation of Poland took its toll on the population. The system whereby 100 Polish hostages were executed for each German killed by the Home Army dissuaded the Polish resistance from overt confrontations with German occupation forces in 1942–44. The Germans used between 50,000 and 80,000 SS-Police and Gestapo to fight a five-year cat and mouse game with the Polish resistance, but failed to destroy it.

One of the early German goals in Warsaw was the eradication of the 400,000 Polish Jews in the city. The Germans created the Warsaw Jewish Ghetto in the autumn of 1940, and in the summer of 1942, the SS began mass deportations from the Warsaw Ghetto to the newly built extermination camps. However, a small group of residents established the Jewish Fighting Organization in order to make

LEFT The Piwna street barricade in Warsaw's Old Town, 24 August 1944. (Peter Dennis © Osprey Publishing)

a last-ditch stand against the SS. The Warsaw Ghetto Uprising began on 19 April 1943 and initially succeeded in evicting the SS troops from the ghetto, but after 28 days the SS finally crushed the last Jewish resistance.

On 23 June 1944 the Soviets launched Operation *Bagration* and quickly shattered the German Army Group Centre. Its remnants fell back into Poland and East Prussia, hotly pursued by the Soviets. Stalin moved rapidly to set up a communist alternative to the Polish Government-in-exile: the Polish Committee of National Liberation, based in the city of Chelm. As Soviet troops drove deeper into Poland and German resistance continued to crumble, the attitude of the Red Army towards the Home Army units it encountered changed from cooperation to overt hostility.

On 27 July, the Soviet 2nd Tank Army routed the German 73rd Infantry Division at Garwolin, driving it back towards Warsaw. Four days later, the 2nd Tank Army was on the outskirts of Warsaw. German support units in the area quickly withdrew across the Vistula River and streamed through Warsaw, reinforcing the Polish impression that the Germans were in full retreat. The hour of liberation seemed at hand.

Although Soviet propaganda normally referred to the Home Army as an 'illegal force', on the night of 29 July, Soviet radio broadcasts urged the Home Army to rise up and overthrow the German garrison in Warsaw. The decision was taken immediately to launch a citywide uprising at 5.00pm on 1 August. Unfortunately, the Polish decision-making was based upon the assumptions that the Germans were about to abandon Warsaw, that the Allies would provide vigorous support to an uprising and that the Soviet offensive would continue. All three assumptions were mistaken.

On 1 August, sporadic clashes began earlier than the planned time, and fighting broke out across the city of Warsaw. On 4 August, the first German reinforcements under SS-Gruppenführer Heinz Reinefarth appeared in the districts of Wola and Ochota. The brutal SS unit led by the notorious SS-Oberführer Oskar Dirlewanger entered Warsaw on the 5th and took part in the Wola Massacre, rounding up and shooting tens of thousands of civilians over the course of two days. On 6 August, Dirlewanger's troops linked up with the encircled German forces in the Bruhl Palace.

German forces began major attacks on the Old Town in Warsaw on 8 August. On 16 August, they captured the water filtration plant, interdicting the city's water supply. The Germans had failed to appreciate the value of denying water and electricity to the city until now, and also failed to realize that the Home Army used the city's sewers to escape German encirclements.

A major Home Army attack from Zoliborz and the Old Town against Gdansk railway station took place on 21 August, but was repulsed with heavy losses. A final Polish attempt to break through to the Old Town from the city centre on 31 August also failed, and on 1–2 September the Home Army units evacuated the Old Town.

Further German attacks and clearances took place from 3 September. On that day, Soviet forces finally resumed their offensive against German forces east of the Vistula, which led the Germans to destroy the bridges over the river. From 16 September, Soviet and US air forces commenced a major resupply operation to the resistance units. However, the German attacks on the Home Army were intensifying, with the capture of the districts of Czerniaków, Mokotów and Zoliborz. On 30 September, Home Army envoys arrived at the German headquarters in the city to begin surrender talks, and the capitulation document was signed on 2 October. The surviving Home Army troops marched out of Warsaw on 4 October, and into captivity.

The terms of surrender stipulated that all civilians would be removed from the city. Out of about 650,000 civilians who were forcibly evicted from Warsaw, about 20 per cent were sent as forced labour to Germany, 15 per cent were sent to concentration camps, and the rest were released to become homeless refugees.

The SS then set about the systematic destruction of Warsaw. Hitler's intent was that the city would simply disappear from the face of Europe – the only time in World War II that the Germans actually tried this on a major city.

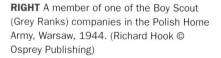

RIGHT A member of one of the Boy Scout (Grey Ranks) companies in the Polish Home Army, Warsaw, 1944. (Richard Hook © Osprey Publishing)

OPERATION *MARKET-GARDEN*

17–25 September 1944

Market-Garden was undoubtedly one of the most ambitious operations of World War II, and the largest airborne operation up to that point. Its failure can be traced chiefly to intelligence misjudgements over whether the German Army was still in the chaotic condition of early September when the operation was planned. In the end, *Market-Garden* was not only 'a bridge too far' but 'two weeks too late.'

September 1944 offered new opportunities to the Allied advance. The slow, steady war of attrition that had marked June, July and August had given way to a war of movement against shattered and retreating German forces. Field Marshal Montgomery's British 21st Army Group had captured the great port of Antwerp intact, and throughout the rest of Belgium and the Netherlands German troops were in retreat with such speed that the withdrawal had almost degenerated into a rout. The widespread expectation was that the war would be over by Christmas.

LEFT US paratrooper assault over the Waal River at Nijmegen, 20 September 1944. (Steve Noon © Osprey Publishing)

In mid-September, Montgomery proposed a bold scheme to accelerate the German collapse. Allied airborne divisions would land behind the German defence in the Netherlands, securing a path for an armoured advance from the Belgian border to the Rhine River at Arnhem. The British tank columns would then be able to cross the Rhine, avoiding the Westwall defensive belt, and strike into Germany's industrial heartland in the neighbouring Ruhr. The resultant Operation *Market-Garden* was in fact two separate, mutually supporting ones; *Market* was the plan to drop British and American airborne troops, and *Garden* was the armoured drive by XXX Corps to meet up with these troops and relieve the airborne lodgement at Arnhem.

For *Garden*, the British XXX Corps would start 21km south of Eindhoven. The Guards Armoured Division would advance northwards along a single road that led to Arnhem through the major towns of Eindhoven, Veghel, Grave and Nijmegen. The crossing points over various canals and the major bridges over the Maas and Waal rivers would by then have been captured by the American paratroopers.

The US airborne objectives for *Market* were to capture the key locations along XXX Corps' route and to hold the road open until relieved by ground troops. The mission given to Major-General Robert E. Urquhart's British 1st Airborne Division in *Market* was the most difficult of all: capturing the furthest bridges over the Rhine River in the city of Arnhem. The 1st Airlanding and 1st Parachute Brigades would land about 10km west of Arnhem, and then the parachute brigade would make a dash to secure the road and rail bridges in the city, with the concrete and steel road bridge being the main objective. A second and a third wave of parachute and glider landings would take place over the following two days. Having driven up from the south, ground troops of British XXX Corps would then relieve the besieged British and Polish airborne troops in the Arnhem bridgehead.

Operation *Market* opened on 17 September with the first wave of landings by the British 1st Airborne Division near Arnhem followed by the airborne landings of the US 101st Airborne Division close to Eindhoven, and by the US 82nd Airborne Division near Nijmegen. That same day, Operation *Garden* got under way with a preparatory barrage and the advance into the Netherlands by the Guards Armoured Division of British XXX Corps. By the evening, Lieutenant-Colonel John Frost's 2nd Parachute Battalion had managed

to capture the northern end of the road bridge at Arnhem, but attempts to secure the southern approaches to the bridge ended in failure.

The following day, 18 September, German opposition at Arnhem prevented the reinforcement of Frost's battalion at the Arnhem bridge. The second wave of landings at Arnhem took place, and the British airborne units were fed piecemeal into the battle to deal with increasing enemy resistance. Meanwhile, by nightfall elements of XXX Corps had met up with paratroopers from the US 101st Airborne Division and reached Eindhoven.

On 19 September, the Germans launched several counter-attacks against the Arnhem bridge; this prevented any hope of reinforcing Frost's slim hold on the northern end, which was being constantly shelled. That same day, the British Guards Armoured Division crossed the rebuilt bridge over the Son Canal and resumed the advance along the main highway, reaching the captured Grave bridge.

On 20 September, German infantry backed by armour managed to surround the British 1st Airborne Division at Arnhem, forcing it into a small pocket at Oosterbeek. Frost's men at the bridge were now completely cut off. Meanwhile a major engagement was developing at Nijmegen: the Guards Armoured Division and the US 82nd Airborne Division combined to capture the city and its two bridges (one road, one rail) over the Waal River. This put them only 16km south of Arnhem.

Early on 21 September, the Germans captured the northern end of the road bridge at Arnhem and eliminated Frost's battalion. That same day, Polish paratroopers from the 1st Parachute Brigade landed south of the Lower Rhine near Driel. Also on the 21st, the attempts by XXX Corps to advance between Nijmegen and Arnhem were halted by the Germans at Elst. During the night of 22/23 September, German attacks managed to cut XXX Corps' highway in the rear at Veghel, preventing forward movement for 40 hours.

Attempts continued to reinforce the airborne lodgement at Arnhem. A small party of the Polish airborne troops at Driel were ferried over the Lower Rhine to join the isolated British troops on the 23rd, while the following day, the 4th Dorsets managed to get two companies across the river.

With the situation untenable, early on 25 September the order was given to evacuate the survivors of the British 1st Airborne Division from Oosterbeek during the hours of darkness. The defeat of the British 1st Airborne Division in Arnhem had doomed the overall campaign, since, without the Rhine bridge at Arnhem, the overall objective of the campaign became meaningless. Only 2,398 survivors made it across the river to join up with friendly forces.

For the Germans, September 1944 would later be called 'the miracle along the Westwall'. The western front was finally stabilized by creating a significant number of new divisions and battle groups that helped blunt the Allies' race to the German frontier.

RIGHT A demolition platoon paratrooper of the US 82nd Airborne Division during Operation *Market-Garden*. (Mike Chappell © Osprey Publishing)

THE BATTLE OF HÜRTGEN FOREST

19 September–16 December 1944

The US Army's campaign in late 1944 and early 1945 against the Siegfried Line (the western defensive frontier of Hitler's Third Reich) was one of the most frustrating and costly efforts in the European theatre. It reached its crescendo in the hellish, prolonged fighting for the Hürtgen Forest.

The Allies began encountering the Siegfried Line in September 1944 after pursuing the retreating Wehrmacht through Belgium and the Netherlands. The terrain was well suited to defence, being a mixture of industrial towns, rivers, hills and forests such as the Reich and Hürtgen. Moreover, the autumn of 1944 was unusually wet; almost double the usual quantity of rain fell. The mud dampened the chances for Allied mechanized operations and the overcast skies constrained air-support operations.

While all of the major Allied formations were involved at one time or another in fighting against the Siegfried Line defences, the battles fought by Lieutenant-General Courtney

LEFT A typical German defence line in the Hürtgen Forest, September 1944. (Steve Noon © Osprey Publishing)

Hodges' US First Army in the Hürtgen Forest epitomize the grim battles along the German frontier. Artillery was the main killer on both sides, and the US infantry was at a distinct disadvantage, being far more vulnerable to artillery air-bursting in the trees overhead than the defending German infantry in log-protected dugouts.

The US 9th Infantry Division was tasked with securing the Roer River crossings at Düren, which lay on the other side of the Hürtgen Forest. The 9th's attack into the forest began on 19 September with a push through the western part of the woods. However, the attack stalled after reaching the open ridgeline that controlled the road from Hürtgen, through Kleinhau and Grosshau, which provided access to the Roer plain in front of Düren. The stubborn German defence and the treacherous wooded terrain meant that by 16 October, the 9th Infantry had advanced only 2.7km, having suffered some 4,500 casualties.

A brief pause ensued, before the Allies launched Operation *Queen*, a broad-front attack aimed at bringing the Allied forces up to the Roer in anticipation of a subsequent push to the Rhine. Part of the planning for *Queen* involved a controversial preliminary operation to push through the towns in the centre of the Hürtgen Forest. This had several tactical goals: it was the first step in clearing a pathway to the key road junction at Düren and providing the US First Army with tactical manoeuvre room beyond the constricted Stolberg corridor; and it would serve to undermine lingering German defence of the Monschau area by threatening them from the rear. The Hürtgen operation was scheduled to be launched on 2 November, three days before the main assault, so that once the mission was completed, another attack could be launched through the town of Hürtgen, and then northwards to Düren.

Since the 9th Infantry Division was spent, the corps boundaries were shifted, with General Leonard T. Gerow's V Corps taking over the Hürtgen sector and substituting the 28th Infantry Division for the 9th Infantry Division.

The 28th Infantry Division was reinforced with a tank battalion attached, but the terrain was not suited to armoured vehicles, with deep ravines and narrow trails. Its three infantry regiments covered a front about 5km wide, and each was assigned a separate mission. The northernmost regiment, the 109th Infantry, was assigned to push north towards Hürtgen as a feint and to secure a launch point for a subsequent attack on Hürtgen. The 112th Infantry Regiment in the centre was assigned to launch the main attack: a two-pronged drive through Vossenack with the second thrust pushing south-east to capture Schmidt. The 110th Infantry Regiment to the south was assigned to push into the clearing east of Lammersdorf in order to secure roads to eventually reinforce and supply the 112th Infantry in Schmidt, since there were hardly any useful roads between Vossenack and Schmidt aside from a single dirt trail up the sides of the Kall River ravine.

The 28th launched its attack on 2 November, but quickly became bogged down in the mud, minefields, intense defensive fire and a succession of German counter-attacks. Little progress was made, and the 28th suffered large numbers of casualties in its efforts. The plan underestimated the German defensive potential in the woods and the difficulties of conducting infantry operations in the mountainous forest.

By mid-November, the US Army's senior leaders were finally aware of the threat posed by the Roer dams, and were determined to gain control of them as well as obtain another route to Düren. Yet the difficulties of forest fighting had still not been fully realized by them, in spite of the horrible costs inflicted on the US 9th and 28th Divisions in the previous fighting.

The Hürtgen sector during Operation *Queen* would see the US VII Corps clearing the northern half of the forest between Schevenhütte and Hürtgen. It would then take Hürtgen and advance to the Roer River just south of Düren. The attack began on 16 November, with the US 4th Infantry Division bearing the brunt of the fighting. In the first three days of the advance, the US 22nd Infantry Regiment lost all three battalion commanders, half its company commanders and many other combat leaders. The advance soon ground to a halt.

The US V Corps joined the fighting on 21 November. US infantry began attacking into the town of Hürtgen on 27 November, while the German Fortress Machine-Gun Battalion 31 continued to defend from the rubble. Finally, on 28 November, a company of infantry rushed the town, riding M4 tanks of the 709th Tank Battalion. House-to-house fighting ensued, but by the end of the day the town was finally in the hands of the 121st Infantry Regiment and 200 prisoners were rounded up.

By the beginning of December, the First Army had fought its way through the Hürtgen Forest, but at a horrible cost.

Combat casualties in the four divisions most heavily involved totalled 23,000 dead, wounded, captured and missing, plus an additional 8,000 men incapacitated by trench foot, combat fatigue and disease. The Wehrmacht lost over 12,000 killed in the forest fighting and many more prisoners and wounded.

Overall, the conduct of the bloody campaign in the Hürtgen was clumsy. The US First Army was unable to exit the forest with enough strength to push on to Düren, and the offensive failed to solve the problem posed by the Roer dams. However, the launch of the Ardennes Offensive on 16 December would put a quick end to the Roer fighting, as the Wehrmacht struck with two armies against the US V Corps' five divisions in what became known as the Battle of the Bulge.

LEFT The Hürtgen Forest terrain was littered with German booby traps and mines, such as the Schrapnellmine 35 or 'S'-mine, shown here. (Peter Dennis © Osprey Publishing)

THE BATTLE OF THE BULGE

16 December 1944–25 January 1945

The Battle of the Bulge – Hitler's last great offensive on the Western Front – drove a wedge into the Allied lines in the Ardennes and caught US forces there completely by surprise. In the ensuing weeks, some 10,000 American prisoners would be taken, the largest surrender of US forces since Bataan in the Philippines in 1942.

In the autumn of 1944, the Ardennes was a 'ghost front' with little combat. The US First Army used the area to rest battle-weary infantry divisions and to acquaint green divisions with life at the front. In mid-December, there were five infantry divisions in the Ardennes: the 2nd and 99th Divisions in the north, the 106th and 28th Divisions in the centre, and the 4th Division further to the south. Elements of the green 9th Armored Division were in reserve to the rear.

The idea for the Ardennes offensive had come to Hitler in mid-September 1944, and he convinced himself that a success in the West could change the course of the war. The offensive (titled *Wacht am Rhein*) was aimed at the sector most weakly held by the US Army, from Monschau in the north to Echternach in the south, a distance of about 60km.

Wacht am Rhein would be conducted by three armies: two panzer armies in the north and centre, and a relatively weak infantry army on the southern flank to block counter-attacks against this shoulder. Hitler assigned his favoured Sixth SS-Panzer Army (led by SS-Oberstgruppenführer Josef 'Sepp' Dietrich) to the attack in the northern sector, which would attack towards Monschau, Höfen, Krinkelt-Rocherath and then Elsenborn Ridge: this was the most important, since success here would secure the shortest route over the Meuse through Liège to the ultimate goal of Antwerp. The northern thrust contained almost two-thirds of the German armoured strength. The Fifth Panzer Army (under General Hasso von Manteuffel) would spearhead a parallel attack in the centre towards St Vith and Bastogne. The weakest of the attacking German armies, the Seventh Army (under General Erich Brandenberger), would strike towards Luxembourg on the southern flank.

LEFT Two M4 medium tanks conduct a rear-guard action on the outskirts of St Vith, 21 December 1944. (Howard Gerrard © Osprey Publishing)

In the Sixth SS-Panzer Army sector, Hitler wanted two special operations to seize vital bridges over the Meuse before they could be destroyed by retreating American forces. Operation *Greif*, led by Hitler's favourite adventurer SS-Obersturmbannführer Otto Skorzeny, would consist of a special brigade of English-speaking German troops disguised as Americans, which would surreptitiously make its way through the American lines to capture vital objectives ahead of the main panzer force. Operation *Stösser* was a paratroop drop to seize vital objectives deep behind the American lines while paralyzing any attempts to reinforce the northern sector: it would end in total failure.

Wacht am Rhein would be strongly affected by weather and terrain conditions. On the one hand, early December was overcast, which limited Allied air reconnaissance before the offensive began, and Allied air attacks after the attack started; but this also meant that Luftwaffe attempts to provide air support for the offensive would be frustrated. The autumn weather in Belgium had been wetter than usual and the soil was saturated and muddy. This severely limited German mobility on the ground, since vehicles, even tanks, became bogged down after they left the roads.

When the offensive was launched, in the northern sector, the Sixth SS-Panzer Army's attack towards Liège was decisively stopped by the defeat of the 12th SS-Panzer Division at Krinkelt-Rocherath and Dom Bütgenbach, and the destruction of the spearhead of the 1st SS-Panzer Division at La Gleize, which the Americans reinforced on 19 December using the US 82nd Airborne Division. Throughout the sector, the German advance had been slowed by stiff American resistance, preventing them from reaching the Allied supply dumps and road networks further to the west.

In the central sector, Fifth Panzer Army fared better in its attack towards Bastogne and St Vith, and gained considerable ground. Fifth Panzer Army managed to trap two of the regiments of the 106th Infantry Division at the Schnee Eifel, leading to the largest mass surrender of US troops and equipment in Europe in World War II. Having created a massive gap in the American lines, the Fifth Panzer Army inserted two of its panzer divisions to exploit the success. The main problem in this sector was that the breach had not been complete. US forces still held the vital road and rail junction at St Vith, which impeded the full exploitation of the gap since it made it difficult to reinforce the spearhead units. US forces successfully defended the St Vith salient from German attacks for six days. The delay that this caused gave the Allied 12th Army Group time to shift additional forces into the Ardennes. The American troops in the salient at St Vith finally withdrew on 23 December.

During the second week of the Ardennes fighting, Hitler attempted to redeem his failing offensive by exploiting the success of the Fifth Panzer Army. Panzer divisions formerly assigned to Sixth SS-Panzer Army were shifted towards the rupture in the centre. Although the panzer spearheads managed to penetrate deep behind the American lines and almost reach the Meuse River, precious time had been lost and the arriving American armoured reinforcements stiffened the Allied resistance.

In the south, Brandenberger's Seventh Army made limited progress and was held up at Bastogne by stubborn American defence. The Americans in the town were soon reinforced by paratroopers of the US 101st Airborne Division, and subsequently by US Third Army's 4th Armored Division. The siege of the vital road junction was lifted on 26 December.

The initiative had by now shifted to the American side and it was no longer a question of whether the German offensive would be defeated, but simply of when. The Allies launched devastating air raids against the German forces, and in a series of hard-fought battles before the Meuse in the final days of 1944, the panzer divisions were decimated and the Ardennes attack was decisively halted. Nevertheless, with the onset of harsh winter weather, it would take a month to finally erase the 'bulge'.

Hitler's final gamble in the West failed within its first week when Sixth SS-Panzer Army was unable to secure the Meuse River bridges at Liège. The stubborn American defence of St Vith turned the eventual advance of the German Panzer units into a 'charge to nowhere' that neither destroyed significant US forces nor secured vital terrain.

RIGHT This SS-Schütze is armed with a captured M1 carbine and has also 'liberated' some American Lucky Strike cigarettes. (Ron Volstad © Osprey Publishing)

THE BATTLE OF IWO JIMA

19 February–26 March 1945

The Battle of Iwo Jima has been described as 'the most savage and most costly battle in the history of the Marine Corps.' Over 70,000 men from three US Marine divisions (the 3rd, 4th and 5th) pitted themselves against more than 21,000 deeply entrenched Japanese troops under Lieutenant-General Tadamichi Kuribayashi. Only 216 Japanese troops would survive to be taken prisoner. For the first time in the Pacific, at Iwo Jima the number of American casualties outstripped those of the Japanese.

The unique strategic location of Iwo Jima made it imperative that the island should come under American control. With the construction of five huge airfields 1,500 miles from the Japanese mainland in the Marianas, the way was open for the US 20th Air Force to mount a massive campaign against the industrial heartland of Japan. However, the only obstacle on the flight path was Iwo Jima. It housed two airfields with a third under construction, and

LEFT US Marines land on Iwo Jima, 19 February 1945.
(Jim Laurier © Osprey Publishing)

a radar station that could give Japan two hours' warning of any impending raid.

Iwo Jima is some 7.25km long with its axis running from south-west to north-east, tapering from 4km wide in the north to a mere 0.8km in the south, giving a total land area of around 19.4km^2. At the southern end stands Mount Suribachi, a 168m-high dormant volcano that affords commanding views over most of the island. The beaches that stretch northwards from Suribachi were the only possible sites for an American landing.

The plan was for the US Marines to land on the 3km-long stretch of beach between Mount Suribachi and the East Boat Basin on the south-east coast of the island. Once landed, the 28th Regiment would attack straight across the narrowest part of the island to the opposite coast, swing left, and isolate and then secure Mount Suribachi. On their right, the 27th Regiment would also cross the island and move to the north, while the 23rd Regiment would seize Airfield No. 1 and then thrust northward towards Airfield No. 2.

The Japanese High Command had realized the strategic importance of Iwo Jima and, as early as March 1944, had begun to reinforce the island. Alongside infantry and armour reinforcements, additional anti-aircraft, mortar, cannon and machine-gun battalions were drafted in. A complex and extensive system of tunnels, caves, gun emplacements, pillboxes and command posts was constructed in the nine months prior to the invasion. Kuribayashi insisted there would be no futile efforts: the Japanese general had realized that attempts to halt the Americans at the beachhead, and suicide charges, invariably failed, but was determined to exact a fearful toll in Marine casualties.

On 15 February 1945, the American invasion fleet left Saipan, first the LSTs carrying the first waves of troops from the 4th and 5th Marine Divisions and the following day the troop transports with the remainder of the Marines and the plethora of tanks, supplies, artillery and supporting units. As a prelude to the landings, three continuous days of shelling by US battleships and cruisers took place against Iwo Jima, to soften up the Japanese defences.

D-Day – Monday, 19 February 1945 – dawned clear and sunny with unlimited visibility. As the Americans hit the landing beaches, the Marines, LVTs, tanks and other vehicles encountered the challenging 4.5m-high terraces of soft black volcanic ash. The troops sank up to their ankles, the vehicles to their hubcaps, and the LVTs and Sherman tanks ground to a halt within yards of the shore. As the first waves of Marines struggled to move forward, successive waves arrived at intervals of around five minutes. The situation rapidly deteriorated when, a little after 10.00am, a torrent of Japanese artillery, mortar and machine-gun fire began to rain down on the crowded beaches. Naval Construction Battalions eventually managed to bulldoze passages up the slopes, and by mid-morning the Marines began extricating themselves from the crowded landing beaches.

The following day, the US 28th Regiment began the unenviable task of capturing Mount Suribachi. After days of bitter fighting, it eventually succeeded in doing so on 23 February, and the American flag was famously raised on its summit. The photograph taken by Associated Press cameraman Joe Rosenthal became arguably the most famous picture of World War II.

To the north the remainder of the invasion force attacked the airfields, with No.1 captured that day (No. 2 fell on 23 February). As the second day drew to a close the Marines had control of almost a quarter of the island, but the cost had been very heavy.

As the three Marine divisions fought their way slowly northwards through Iwo Jima, the 4th Division came up against a complex of four formidable defence positions to the east of Airfield No. 2 that became known as 'the Meatgrinder'. The complex comprised Hill 382, Turkey Knob, the Amphitheater and the ruins of Minami Village. This would be the scene of some of the bloodiest actions of the whole battle. Eventually, the grinding head-on assaults of the Marines won out, and the last Japanese resistance in the Meatgrinder was finally cleared on 15 March.

Although General Kuribayashi had forbidden wasteful suicide charges, on 8 March Captain Samaji Inouye and 1,000 of his men launched a night-time 'banzai' attack in an effort to retake Mount Suribachi. Around midnight, they advanced towards the US Marine front line. By the light of star shells, the Japanese died in their hundreds under a barrage of artillery, machine-gun and small-arms fire.

During the final week of the campaign, the Japanese forces were split in two at the northern end of the island, and became confined to three distinct pockets. General Kuribayashi and the remains of his command were entrenched in a place known as Death Valley on the north-west coast. Kuribayashi was probably killed when his cave complex was destroyed on 21 March, although his body was never found.

Iwo Jima was officially declared secure at 9.00am on 26 March 1945, although it would take three months to mop up the final isolated Japanese defenders holed up across the island. Two Japanese soldiers (Yamakage Kufuku and Matsudo Linsoki) even managed to hold out for four years, finally surrendering on 6 January 1949.

LEFT The US Navy and USMC Medal of Honor, the highest award for bravery that the US can bestow on a member of its military. (Ramiro Bujeiro © Osprey Publishing)

THE BATTLE OF OKINAWA

1 April–22 June 1945

Okinawa was the largest sea, land and air battle in history, and witnessed the largest amphibious landing carried out by American forces during the Pacific Campaign. The logistical effort to mount and sustain such a massive campaign was enormous.

The spring of 1945 found Allied fortunes in the Pacific very much in the ascendant. Many of the islands and territories seized by the Imperial Japanese forces had been reclaimed, and there was no doubt that the Allies would be the ultimate victors. For the Japanese, the only question remaining was where the Allies would strike next. The Imperial General Headquarters narrowed the possible targets to Formosa off the Chinese mainland, or Okinawa south-west of the Home Islands. The Japanese began to reinforce both areas as the American Fifth Fleet and Tenth Army marshalled at island bases across the Pacific.

LEFT The US 193rd Tank Battalion and the Japanese 272nd Independent Infantry Battalion fight for Kakazu Ridge, 19 April 1945. (Howard Gerrard © Osprey Publishing)

The Allies planned an invasion of Okinawa (codenamed *Iceberg*) as the last operation before a November 1945 invasion of Japan itself. The island is the largest of the 161 islands in the Ryukyus chain, and lies only 515km south-west of the Japanese home island of Kyushu. Its southern end was where most of the 435,000 inhabitants lived, including thousands of Japanese immigrants.

The main landing would begin at 8.30am, 1 April 1945 (H-Hour, L-Day). The largest simultaneous amphibious assault in the Pacific War would see the landing of two Marine and two Army divisions abreast on 12.8km of beach. The US divisions would then head rapidly inland, in order to sever the island at the narrow Ishikawa Isthmus. Once completed, the Japanese forces would be divided and isolated, allowing US forces to focus on the main objective of the island's southern end.

Over 1,300 Allied ships were committed to Operation *Iceberg*. Task Force 51 contained elements from the US Army, Navy, Marine Corps and the three services' air arms; its role was to transport and deliver the American landing forces, sustain them ashore, provide air cover and close air support, and deliver naval gunfire support. The carriers and aircraft of Task Force 58 and the British Task Force 57 also took part in the operation, preparing to engage any remnants of the Japanese Navy that might attempt to sortie.

The landings began as planned on 1 April, with the US Tenth Army assaulting Okinawa's Hagushi beaches with four divisions. There was little initial resistance ashore, and in the first hour 50,000 troops were landed. The US 4th Marines and 17th Infantry Regiments managed to reach the key airfields at Yontan and Kaden three days ahead of schedule. The following day, the rapid advance continued and forward elements of the US 7th Infantry Division reached the east coast, severing the island; the two airfields were also secured. Still there was little response from the Japanese.

On 4 April, the US 7th and 96th Infantry Divisions pushed south and the first heavy resistance was encountered on Cactus, Kaniku and Tombstone Ridges. It was at this point that the outlying positions of the Japanese Shuri defences were uncovered. This was the main Japanese defensive position on the island, and was centred on Shuri Castle and a vast, rugged cross-island ridge and hill complex. The American advance began to encounter very tough resistance,

and the fighting to overcome the Shuri defences would be bitter, slow and costly.

At sea, the first two weeks of the campaign saw the Allied carriers executing attacks throughout the Ryukyus, and on Formosa, mainland China and Kyushu to neutralize Japanese airfields. The American and British Task Forces were subject to multiple *kamikaze* attacks throughout the operation, notably on 6–7 April when a massive 355-plane raid was unleashed. These attacks would continue through May and into late June, resulting in 26 US ships sunk and 225 damaged.

In a desperate effort the Japanese sortied the battleship *Yamato* on 6 April on a suicide mission, departing from Honshu in Japan. The super battleship was to beach itself on Okinawa in order to bombard American forces ashore and the transports. However, halfway to Okinawa, Allied Task Force 58 aircraft sank the *Yamato*, which went down with 2,487 crew.

Between 4 and 6 May, the Japanese 24th Division launched a major counter-attack against the US 77th and 7th Infantry Divisions on Okinawa. The aim was to seize the Tanabaru escarpment and then the Futema–Atanniya–Atsuta area, on the second narrowest neck of the island, in order to contain the US Tenth Army. The US XXIV Corps managed to repulse this attack.

Between 13 and 19 May 1945, the 6th Marine Division assaulted Sugar Loaf Hill, the key to breaching the west flank of the Shuri defences. It took seven days to advance 520 yards. More than 3,000 Marines and untold thousands of Japanese were killed or wounded in the fighting there.

On 31 May, the 5th Marines managed to occupy the main Japanese defensive positions. Shuri Castle itself housed the Japanese 32nd Army's headquarters in underground tunnels, and control of it was hotly contested. The remnants of the Japanese 32nd Army began to withdraw from the Shuri defences south to their final positions in the Kiyamu Peninsula, although substantial pockets remained in the American rear areas.

The last remaining Japanese resistance on the island was largely wiped out by 21 June, with Okinawa declared secure at 5.00pm that day. Mopping up would continue for several days, in the course of which the surviving Japanese officers either committed ritual suicide or launched 'honourable death' attacks.

The 82-day-long, no-quarter battle for Okinawa had resulted in very high numbers of casualties. Marine ground and air losses were 2,938 dead and missing and 16,017 wounded. The US Army lost 4,675 dead and missing and 18,099 wounded. There were over 26,200 US casualties due to combat fatigue, illness and non-battle injuries. The joint US air services lost 763 aircraft, and the US Navy saw 36 ships sunk. An estimated 66,000 Japanese combatants died during the battle for Okinawa, and around 7,400 were taken prisoner. Over 120,000 civilians also perished – a figure equalling the combined death toll at Hiroshima and Nagasaki.

RIGHT The F6F-5 Hellcat flown by Lieutenant Eugene Valencia of VF-9 from USS *Yorktown* (CV-10), April 1945. (Jim Laurier © Osprey Publishing)

THE BATTLE OF BERLIN

16 April–2 May 1945

The Battle of Berlin provided a conclusive end to the fighting in the European theatre. The Soviet assault on the capital of Nazi Germany and the heart of the Third Reich was the culmination of a remorseless effort by Stalin's forces to push the Germans out of the USSR and then westwards out of Eastern Europe.

The final Soviet offensive to crush Nazi Germany began on 12 January 1945. Warsaw quickly fell, and by 20 January, the Soviets had broken through along a 350-mile front and had taken Krakow and Lodz in Poland. By early February 1945, the Soviets had reached the Oder River, less than 80km from the German capital. The stage was set for the final Soviet push to capture Berlin.

For Stalin, Berlin was the major prize, and he feared that the Red Army might be beaten to it by Montgomery's 21st Army Group, which was advancing rapidly from Holland into North Germany. The British had always viewed Berlin as the

LEFT Soviet troops of the 79th Rifle Corps attack the Reichstag, 30 April 1945. (Peter Dennis © Osprey Publishing)

central objective and had envisaged that Montgomery would make the main thrust to the north and east. However, Allied Supreme Commander Eisenhower effectively demolished this by continuing to plan for an offensive that concentrated the Western Allies' advance in the centre in order to meet the Soviet advance around Dresden and cut Germany in two. Berlin had little significance for him.

The Soviet plan for Operation *Berlin* was formed on 1 April. To the north, the 2nd Byelorussian Front under Marshal Rokossovsky, which was still engaged in East Prussia, would continue its advance westward to the north of Berlin as soon as it was practicable. Marshal Zhukov's 1st Byelorussian Front (located 80km directly east of Berlin) and Marshal Ivan Konev's 1st Ukrainian Front (positioned further south) would assault Berlin directly. Further to the south, the 4th and 2nd Ukrainian Fronts would continue to advance into Czechoslovakia, while the 3rd Ukrainian Front would continue to drive west through Hungary and into Austria.

German preparations to heavily fortify Berlin had been underway since March 1945. A series of obstacle belts, defensive lines and inner and outer rings were established around the city, with an innermost 'Citadel' around the most important Nazi governmental buildings such as the Reichstag and Reich Chancellery. The defensive areas would be split into various sectors, where it was intended that German forces would conduct a defence in depth.

At 5.00am on 16 April 1945, Operation *Berlin* began with an enormous artillery barrage on the forward German lines defending the Seelow Heights, which comprised the last defensible region to the east of Berlin. After about 20 minutes, 143 searchlights were turned on to blind the defenders and light the way for the Soviet assault formations, while the barrage moved on deeper into the German positions. Zhukov's forces managed to clear the first line of German defences, but another line was on top of the Seelow Heights. Zhukov failed to identify the German main line of resistance here and had to battle for four days in order to break through at a cost of over 30,000 Soviet dead.

Konev's 1st Ukrainian Front began its advance on Berlin at the same time as Zhukov's forces, crossing the Neisse River at over 150 sites. His forces pushed rapidly west to reach the Elbe River and then drove north against little resistance to encircle Berlin from the south. On 20 April, Rokossovsky's 2nd Byelorussian Front began its offensive across the lower Vistula River in the north, driving back the German Army Group Vistula and pushing west to the Baltic coast.

To the east of Berlin, the remnants of General Theodor Busse's German Ninth Army found itself pressed on all sides by Zhukov's advance, and by 24 April had been driven into a pocket in the Spree Forest south of the Seelow Heights. Busse attempted to break out to the west and join up with the German Twelfth Army, but his army was destroyed piecemeal, with the survivors trickling back west to avoid Soviet captivity.

The Soviet advance now proceeded rapidly. By 25 April, Berlin had been completely encircled by the fronts of Konev and Zhukov. To the west on the Elbe River, Konev's 5th Guards Army and troops from the US First Army linked up near Torgau, the first Soviet–American forces to do so.

On 26 April, the German Twelfth Army, west of Berlin, launched a counter-attack through Konev's forces in an effort to reach the capital, but was too weak to break through. The encircling Soviet formations began to work their way into the Berlin suburbs to the north and the east, learning the techniques of urban fighting as they went. By the end of 27 April, the Soviet 5th Shock Army was only 3km from the Reich Chancellery. The area around the Reichstag was heavily defended, with many of the buildings turned into veritable fortresses, and substantial bodies of German troops hampered the Soviets' forward progress using tank-hunting teams. Soviet acts of revenge for the Germans' treatment of civilians and property in the Soviet Union were becoming commonplace, with looting, rape and, occasionally, murder the order of the day in many places.

In the 'Citadel' within the German capital, the imminence of defeat was now apparent. On 29 April, Hitler married Eva Braun and prepared his last will and testament, and the following day they committed suicide at around 3.20pm. The Soviets assaulted the Reichstag building throughout the day, and after intense fighting finally raised the Red Flag on its roof at 10.50pm.

The news of Hitler's death was broadcast to the German people on 1 May by the new head of government, Admiral Karl Dönitz. The following day, Soviet troops stormed the Reich Chancellery, and the Berlin Garrison surrendered on the orders of General Helmuth Weidling. It proved difficult for the Soviets to immediately bring their troops under control, and numerous atrocities were visited on the civilian population in the days that followed. The unconditional surrender of Nazi Germany was eventually finalized in the late evening of 8 May 1945, bringing to an end the European fighting of World War II.

RIGHT A junior lieutenant in the Red Army armed with the Tokarev pistol, Berlin, 1945. (Ron Volstad © Osprey Publishing)

INDEX